in retrospect

by chris d. baker

foreword by jerry h. geib

The Donning Company/Publishers
184 Business Park Drive, Suite 106
Virginia Beach, Virginia 23462

This book was produced under the auspices of the
Ottumwa Public Library in conjunction with an Iowa
Community Cultural Grant awarded by the Iowa
Department of Cultural Affairs.

Nancy Schneiderheinze, Project Director

Library of Congress Cataloging-in-Publication Data

Baker, Chris D., 1956-
      In retrospect / by Chris D. Baker.
             p. cm.
      Includes bibliographical references and index.
      ISBN 0-89865-842-X (hardcover:alk. paper)
      1. Wapello County (Iowa)—History—Pictorial works. I. Title.
F627.W2B35   1992
  977.7'93—dc20   92-12034
                                                  CIP

Printed in the United States of America

this book is dedicated to
betty durham and
the late raymond d. baker

*The publication of this book was
made possible by these local sponsors:*

**FIRSTAR Bank Ottumwa
McCune & Reed Insurance
NOEL Insurance, Inc.
Norwest Bank Iowa
South Ottumwa Savings Bank**

preface

Collecting and assembling the images of the past into a single, coherent vision is a trying and consuming process. The primary concerns are assessing which images and bits of information should be included or excluded, and how to present the same in a manageable and palatable format. Thus, this book covers slightly more than the first 100 years of Wapello County, which is prefaced by an overview of Native American history leading up to 1843, the year the county was rushed by settlers. The ending year is 1947, the last time the meandering Des Moines River surged over its banks before engineers straightened the river channel in the 1950s.

I have spent much of the past year rummaging through stacks of photographs at the Ottumwa Public Library and the Wapello County Historical Society, as well as visiting the homes of Wapello County residents eager to share family histories, recollections, memorabilia and, of course, photographs. Their contribution to this effort is immeasurable. More than six hundred photographs were copied for possible publication. Unfortunately, it is impossible to include all of the images. Whenever possible, I have tried to select photographs of identifiable subjects, but that is not an absolute prerequisite for inclusion. Some photographs of unidentified people are used because their contents depict relevant information unique to specific time periods. The same logic applies to photographs of questionable physical condition. The images, many of which are from private collections and are being published for the first time, are indexed and available for viewing at the Ottumwa Public Library.

This book does not represent a comprehensive history of Wapello County; it is merely a glimpse into its past. As it is impossible to locate photographs and documents that wholly illustrate a chronology of local events, the information is presented by subject. An attempt has been made to arrange the chapters in an order that reflects the social and economic development of Wapello County, but, because of the interdependent facets within any society, some subject overlap does occur among the respective chapters.

The primary intent behind this book is to provide a photographic history of Wapello County, but relevant illustrations, documents, and text have also been included to complement the images. The text represents an abridged version of local history and is presented only as a thread of continuity between the images. Several excellent references are available at the Ottumwa Public Library for persons interested in a complete written history of the county. A bibliography is located in the back of this book.

Although great care has been taken to present a fair picture of Wapello County, it is impossible to discount the subjective eye of an author. My respect is extended to those whose interpretations of the past differ from my own.

Finally, it is important to thank those who helped make this book possible: Ottumwa Library Director Jerry H. Geib, who secured the funding for this project; librarian Mary Ann Lemon, an invaluable editor and researcher; members of the Wapello County Historical Society— specifically, Sue Parrish and Barbara Kramer; Lucille Doughty, who kept a vigilant eye out for photographs; Dr. Hanno Hardt, Associate Professor Kay Amert, Dr. Judy Polumbaum and Steve Siegel, for their considered opinions; members of the Iowa Department of Cultural Affairs, who funded this project with an Iowa Community Cultural Grant; and, the local sponsors.

chris d. baker

table of
contents

An early bicycling enthusiast pedals toward downtown Ottumwa, circa 1890.

foreword

a s Wapello County prepares to celebrate its sesquicenten-
nial anniversary, we are reminded of the essential need for
information about our historical past. Over the past 150 years,
only four principal books have attempted to provide and pre-
serve valuable insight into the rich history of Wapello County. *in
retrospect: an illustrated history of wapello county, iowa* was
brought about by this critical need to add to the distinctly small
body of literature regarding our local history.

The public library, as an institution within the community,
has a clear role to perform in the preservation and dissemination
of information. Local history is a vast assortment of people, ob-
jects, and institutions which illuminate the past. This book represents a first attempt to pull together and emphasize those images
which illustrate that past.

It is an exciting opportunity for the Ottumwa Public Library
to publish a new and different approach to the county's past and,
in turn, supplement existing historical accounts. These pictures

offer striking evidence of the changes that have taken place through the years in the landscape, the texture of the neighborhoods, and the people. By freezing time, they offer style and evidence of communities taking shape, institutions forming and growing, agencies serving and struggling, and businesses prospering and declining.

A photograph is a special kind of document and using it in presenting historical research requires some technical knowledge and expertise. Finding an author who possessed that knowledge was critical to the success of this endeavor. The Ottumwa Public Library was fortunate to find and hire Chris D. Baker for this task. Not only is Baker imminently qualified because of his experience in photography and educational qualifications in journalism, but as a native of Wapello County, he has a deep and abiding interest in the county's history.

None of the above would have been possible without the encouragement and help of so many people. This project began initially because of an Iowa Community Cultural Grant bestowed upon the Ottumwa Public Library by the Iowa Department of Cultural Affairs. It progressed from creating an index of existing history texts, to creating a book for the public, because of the gracious sponsorship of several institutions. They are Firstar Bank, South Ottumwa Savings Bank, Norwest Bank, McCune and Reed Insurance Agency, and Noel Insurance Agency.

in retrospect: an illustrated history of wapello county, iowa is the result of a dedicated and resourceful teamwork of people within the community we label Wapello County. We gratefully acknowledge individual donations of photographic materials from local institutions such as the Wapello County Historical Society and the Wapello County Genealogical Society. We are also indebted to the technical and professional expertise of the Donning Company/Publishers and the many individuals who shared their trust and family treasures with the Ottumwa Public Library.

Historical literature is necessary if we are to understand and appreciate our past. I believe this book represents a first step in that direction. It should remind us all that we not only inherit a great legacy from our ancestors, but that we have a responsibility to promote and build upon that legacy for the next generation. I hope and trust you will enjoy this look at Wapello County's past.

jerry h. geib, director
ottumwa public library

Studio portraits of the past relied on the understated elegance of natural lighting. Pictured is June Edith Davis, circa 1900.

This 1836 map of the Wisconsin Territory, by Lt. Albert M. Lea, includes several Iowa towns. Lea was a surveyor stationed with the U. S. Dragoons.

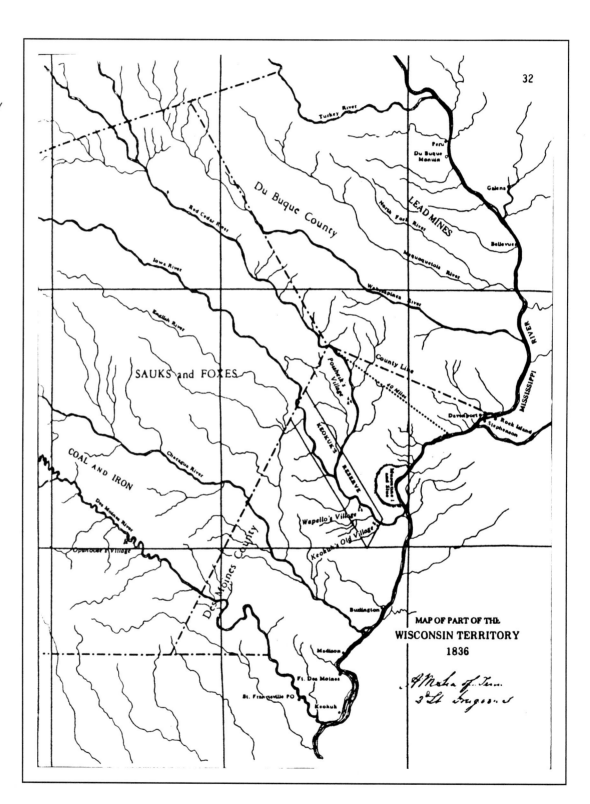

MAP OF PART OF THE
WISCONSIN TERRITORY
1836

early
history

t he modern history of Iowa and, thus, Wapello County, evolves from the 1803 Louisiana Purchase. Before the Terri tory of Iowa was officially recognized in 1838, it was once part of the Wisconsin Territory (see map). Prior to that enactment, Iowa was included in the Michigan, Missouri and New Orleans Territories, respectively.

Originally, the land was inhabited by several Indian tribes including the Iowa, Sioux, Missouri, Otoe, Pawnee, and most notably by members of the united Sac (sometimes spelled Sauk) and Fox nations who moved into the area from northern Illinois and southern Wisconsin.

The latter tribes were not strangers to the U.S. government. In the War of 1812, they sided with the British forces at Detroit. In addition, under the leadership of Chief Black Hawk, a Sac, they attacked Ft. Madison, a U.S. outpost established in 1808. Conflicting reports exist regarding the success of the attack. One early account states that the war party was defeated by a garrison

major land purchases in iowa

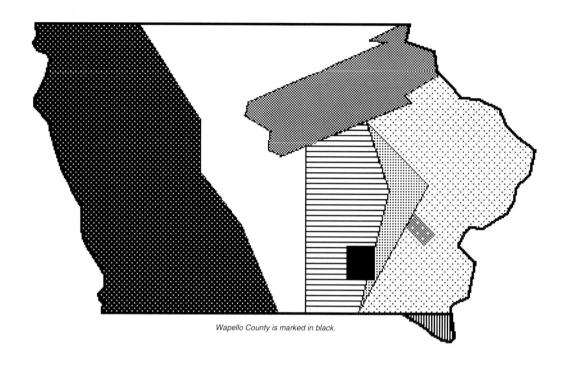

Wapello County is marked in black.

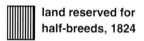 land reserved for half-breeds, 1824   western slope, established 1830

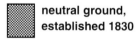 neutral ground, established 1830   chief keokuk's reserve, 1836

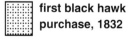 first black hawk purchase, 1832   second black hawk purchase, 1837

final sac and fox cession—1842

Chief Black Hawk, the leader of the Sac and Fox confederacy, died in 1838. He was originally buried in Wapello County, about one mile east of Eldon, near the former town of Iowaville in Van Buren County.

of fifty soldiers. A later version claims that the fort was burned to the ground.

the black hawk war

After the War of 1812, peace treaties were signed in 1815 by most of the tribal chiefs except Black Hawk. His "British" band of Sacs did not acknowledge the pact until one year later, but even then, the chief later claimed that he had been deceived into ceding his village on the Rock River, near what is now Rock Island, Illinois. That contested cession precipitated the Black Hawk War of 1832.

By 1830, as whites continued their push westward, Black Hawk's animosity toward the United States continued to fester. According to early historians, the final indignation occurred when, upon returning from a hunting trip, Black Hawk and his party found white families living in their village wigwams. Black Hawk's own people, forced out of their homes, were living on the banks of the Rock River.

Black Hawk protested the actions of the white settlers and eventually reclaimed his village without bloodshed. Some historians argue that Black Hawk's actions were well within his rights. According to the treaty, in which the Native Americans relinquished ownership to their homeland, the Sacs and Foxes were granted the right to hunt on the land as long it was owned by the United States. Despite that stipulation, displaced white settlers complained to the government and a military force was organized.

Although the Black Hawk War is usually associated with the history of Illinois, it was equally important to the establishment of Iowa and Wapello County. Black Hawk was the recognized leader of the Sac and Fox nation and it was his refusal to bow to the U.S. government that eventually divided the confederacy. This dissension— dating back to the War of 1812— gave rise to the emergence of Keokuk as a rival chief. Keokuk, a favorite of the government, convinced his followers to permanently resettle across the Mississippi River, in what is now Iowa, to avoid the inevitable conflict.

One account credits Keokuk with the following speech intended to underscore the strength of the white military and to pacify his warriors:

"But," said [Keokuk], "if you do determine to go upon the warpath, I will agree to lead you on one condition: that before we go, we will kill all of our old men and our wives and children, to save them from a lingering death of starvation, and that

Nokawata, left, great-grandson of Chief Wapello, visiting his ancestor's grave located near Agency, circa 1930.

Gen. Joseph Street, left, was appointed the area's first Indian agent in 1838. His friend, Chief Wapello, right, for whom the county is named, was Chief Black Hawk's successor as the leader of the Sac and Fox confederate tribes. The graves of the two men, who are buried side by side, can be seen at Chief Wapello Memorial Park.

every one of us determine to leave our homes on the other side of the Mississippi."

As Black Hawk and his band returned time and again to the Rock River village, tensions mounted. Finally, in 1832, despite reported efforts by Black Hawk to establish a truce with the U.S. government, the military was mobilized.

Accounts of the Black Hawk War differ. What some historians cite as a battle, others deplore as a blatant massacre of a starving, fleeing people. One truth is clear— Black Hawk and his band were defeated and the chief was imprisoned. Later he was ordered to the nation's capital and paraded through many eastern cities.

major land purchases in iowa

The 1832 treaty resulting from the war was signed by Keokuk and other members of the Sac and Fox confederacy who ceded a fifty-mile tract of land on the eastern border of Iowa extending from Missouri to the mouth of the Upper Iowa River. Six million acres were obtained by the U.S. government in what is referred to as the Black Hawk Purchase (see map).

A series of treaties followed which eventually pushed the tribes to the Des Moines River and what is now Wapello County. The four hundred square acres known as Keokuk's Reserve was ceded in 1836. One year later, the Sac and Fox sold yet another strip of land officially recognized as the Second Black Hawk Purchase. The final treaty, in which the Sac and Fox relinquished all rights to the land west of the Mississippi River, was signed on Oct. 11, 1842 at the Sac and Fox Indian Agency, near the present town of Agency.

sac and fox indian agency

The Sac and Fox Indian Agency, established in 1838, operated under the supervision of Gen. Joseph M. Street. In the course of his duties, Street befriended Chief Wapello, for whom the county is named, and the two men forged an enduring relationship. Street died in May of 1840. Wapello died two years later about five miles northeast of what is now the town of Ollie in Keokuk County. His request to be buried next to his friend was honored and their graves can still be viewed at Chief Wapello Memorial Park.

The following account of Wapello's death appeared in the Sept. 13, 1876 edition of the Ottumwa *Courier*:

"The name of our county— Wapello— should be pronounced as though spelled *Wappelaw*. At any rate, that is the

The Sac and Fox Indian Agency was built in 1838 under the direction of Gen. Joseph Street. The above structure is all that remained of the original agency when this picture was made, circa 1903. The building was located just southeast of what is now the town of Agency.

way the Chief Wapello pronounced it, and he ought to have known.

"The old chief died at the forks of the Skunk River, March 15, 1842, and his remains were brought to the Indian Agency, near where Agency City is now located, in an ox-wagon, and buried toward evening of the same day, with the customary Indian ceremonies. At his own request, he was buried by the side of Gen. Street, in the garden of the Agency. Gen. Street had been an Indian Agent at Prairie du Chien and at Rock Island. He came to the Agency of the Sac and Fox here in April, 1838, by assignment of the Commissioner of Indian Affairs, Judge Crawford, and died May 5, 1840. He was for many years in the Indian service, and although always a strong Whig, he was yet a man of such sterling integrity that he remained in office until the day of his death, in spite of his politics and the changes in administration. He was very popular with the Indians, and hence the desire of Wapello to be laid side by side of his honest pale-faced friend, which wish was gratified. Gen. Street left numerous children and grandchildren, none of whom reside here now.

"Keokuk, Appanoose and nearly all the leading men among the Indians, were present at Wapello's funeral. The dead chief was the successor of Black Hawk in rank. If Wapello's name is translated in English, we are unacquainted with the fact (*Editor's note: According to one historian, the translation is "He Who Is Painted White."*). He was the chief of the Fox as well as the confederate tribes of Sac and Fox composed of the bands of Keokuk, Appanoose, Hardfish, Poweshiek and his own; Poweshiek succeeded him as the senior chief of the confederate tribes, while Poweshiek's tribe-leadership fell to Pasheshamore (Pa-she-sha-more), who, from all accounts, was a good sort of an Indian. He went to the Indian Territory with the Sac and Fox where the remnants of this dejected race still subsist upon the bounty of the Government."

Following Street's death, his son-in-law, Major John Beach, was appointed his successor. Shortly before his own death in 1874, Beach began to write his version of the history of the Indian agency which was published in part by the Agency *Independent*. His account, too long to be published here in its entirety, includes a wealth of historical anecdotes and is recommended reading for those interested in the early history of the agency and Wapello County. The following passages appear in Beach's chronicle.

indian villages

In describing the locations of the respective Sac and Fox villages, Beach writes:

"At the time of Gen. Street's decease, the Indians were occupying their country with their permanent, or spring and summer villages, located as follows: Upon the bank of the Des Moines, opposite the mouth of Sugar Creek, where there is quite a spacious bottom extending for a mile or more below, where the bluff closes in pretty closely upon the bank, and for a much longer distance in the up-river direction toward and past Ottumwa, was the village of Keokuk; and, still above, were those of Wapello of the Fox and Appanoose, a Sac chief. According to the writer's present memory, that of Wapello was the intermediate one. Keokuk himself, had selected a pleasant, commanding and picturesque point for his own summer wigwam, some halfway up the side of the bluff, in the rear of his village, where, with his own little field of corn and beans, despite the large field of Uncle Sam's just beneath him, he enjoyed the *otium cum*

Maj. John Beach, the son-in-law of Gen. Joseph Street, became the second agent of the Sac and Fox Indian Agency in 1840.

Chief Keokuk's village was near the Des Moines River, opposite the mouth of Sugar Creek.

A page from J. P. Eddy's 1840 trade journal. Eddy's trading post was located at the present site of Eddyville.

dignitate of his authority and rank during the hot weather.

" . . . Several of the lodges in every town had their own patches of cultivated ground in the neighborhood of their villages; but the hillside, now covered by Ottumwa, seemed to offer them more attractive spots for this purpose, probably because the soil was more easily worked, and situated more favorably for the influence of the sun upon their side of the river. A light, easily turned soil was, of course, an object to the poor squaws, upon whom devolved the duty of working it with their hoes, and of inserting the rickety posts, that with light posts bound to them, made the fence, not exceeding four feet in height, but, in general, very respectfully treated by the ponies, the only animal liable to intrude injuriously upon their fields . . .

"The village of Hardfish— or Wishecomaque, as it is in the Indian tongue— which was quite as respectable in size as any of the old villages, was located in what is now the heart of Eddyville, named for J. P. Eddy, a trader, who was licensed in the summer of 1840, by the writer, to establish his trading post at that place. He continued to trade there until the treaty of final cession in 1842, and was the most fortunate of any of the large traders in finding his claims against the Indians very little reduced by the Commissioners, whose part it was, at the treaty, to adjust all outstanding claims against the Sac and Fox.

"The writer cannot locate the place exactly, according to our state maps, although he has often visited it in Indian times; but somewhere out north from Kirkville, and probably not over twelve miles distant, on the bank of the Skunk River, not far above the 'Forks of Skunk,' was a small village of not over fifteen or twenty lodges, preside over by a man of considerable influence, though he was not a chief, named Kishkekosh. The village was on the direct trail— in fact it was the converging point of the two trails— from the Hardfish village, and the three villages across the river below Ottumwa, to the only other permanent settlement of the tribe, which was the village of Poweshiek, a Fox chief of equal rank with Wapello, situated on the bank of the Iowa River."

Chief Appanoose, a Sac, fooled Gen. Street into believing that Sugar Creek, between Ottumwa and Agency, was 50 miles long.

appanoose tricks gen. street

Revealing his sense of humor, Beach also details the antics of Chief Appanoose, a Sac, who, following the 1837 treaty, tricked Gen. Street into a financial blunder:

"Appanoose persuaded Gen. Street that Sugar Creek, between Ottumwa and Agency was fifty miles long, and the general had a mill erected on it. A freshet occurred within the next twelve months or so, sufficient in size and force to wash it away; but the writer doubts if ever a bushel of grain were grounded in it, nor, had it stood to this day, and had the Indians remained to this day, does he believe that they could have been prevailed upon to have raised a bushel of corn to carry to it. Another mill was put up on Soap Creek, and when the writer took charge of the Agency, in June, 1840, that also was destroyed; but as that was a better stream and he was fortunate enough to have secured the services of Mr. Peter Wood, a man who fully understood his business, and was honestly disposed to attend to it, a second mill that was erected fared better, but the Indians took no interest in it whatever."

trade humor

Perhaps the most humorous account in Beach's writings involves Territorial Gov. Robert Lucas, the P. Chouteau Jr. & Co. (a trading company once located three miles from Agency at Garrison Rock), and a cache of lard-filled kegs.

According to Beach, the governor had long suspected that the Chouteau company was illegally selling whisky to the Sac and Fox tribes and he was determined to catch the rascals. Upon learning of Gov. Lucas' intentions, a wry Captain Billy Phelps, employed by the trading company, sent a cohort, named Suggs, to Burlington. Suggs spread the rumor that, indeed, the trading company had just received and buried a new batch of whisky to be sold to the Indians at a later date. Gov. Lucas embraced the rumor and quickly moved to obtain a search warrant. He dispatched his men to the Sac and Fox Indian Agency to enlist the services of Beach, who writes:

"Reaching the trading-house, the person who took the deposition and a companion were found their waiting, they having 'forked off' by another trail as not to be seen. Suggs was on hand, having the opportunity to post the Burlingtonians about the locality. And also Capt. Billy Phelps, called by the Indians Che-che-pe-qua, or the 'Winking Eyes,' was there, those visuals fairly gleaming with joy over the anticipated fun.

"The Agent proceeded at once to business, expressing to Capt. Phelps his regret that so unpleasant a duty should be devolved upon him; his hope that it would prove that so serious a complaint had originated in some error, but suggesting that, if true, admission to the fact and production of the contraband article would be more apt to temper subsequent proceedings with leniency than efforts to conceal it would do. The Captain vehemently denied the impeachment, stating that it would require a

The home of the P. Chouteau Jr. & Co. trading post in the late 1830s was near Garrison Rock. Ft. Sanford, above, was established there in 1842.

much wiser man than himself to discover where such an article then was, or had ever been kept upon their premises. The complainant was now appealed to, who led the party a short distance to a spot where, with a triumphant air, he pointed to an X that the edge of Suggs' boot sole had made in the sandy bank.

"They began digging, and soon reached some matting that was removed, and thus uncovered a lot of lard kegs, too greasy to suggest a thought of any other article being contained within them. The immediate 'sold by thunder!' of one of the moiety gentlemen, came in accents too lugubrious to be listened to without exciting a sense of sadness. Suggs, meanwhile, had come up missing, and the 'Winking Eyes' walked off with a most disdainful air, leaving the Agent and his party on the spot, whence they soon returned to the Agency, where the Agent made his report that the informer had pointed out a place, where, by digging, a large quantity of lard in kegs was found that had been buried to avoid loss by heat, and in the night to conceal the fact from vagabond whites and Indians. The disappointed informer and his companion returned hastened homeward; but Col. Williams remained until next morning, and then returned bearing the Agent's report.

"But the unkindest cut of all was six months later, when, about the last of February, Capt. Phelps addressed a letter to Gov. Lucas in the most respectful manner and official form, saying, that having heard he had declared his determination not to continue in office under such an old Tory as Gen. Harrison, and fearful that whoever his successor would be, he might not feel so friendly toward the Company as he had proved in the matter of exhuming their lard, and as they would soon be much in need of some, and the ground was then very hard frozen, the Company would be under great obligation if he would at once send some one out to dig up the rest of it."

Robert Lucas was appointed the first governor of the Territory of Iowa in 1838.

Early in 1843 preparations were being made to open the area to white settlers, and most of the remaining Sac and Fox, having signed away all of their Iowa land, were removed to Kansas. Unhappy with life in Kansas, small groups began to return to Iowa and were eventually allowed to reside on the settlement near Tama where some of their descendants live today.

The first hewn log cabin in Keokuk Township, Wapello County, was built in 1846 by Benjamin Young.

new
beginnings

a t the stroke of midnight, May 1, 1843, the echo of several carbine reports sounded the cue for more than two thousand settlers to race in and stake their claims in a land recently relinquished by the Sac and Fox tribes.

Since the 1842 treaty prevented any and all homesteaders from entering the new land until the Sac and Fox had resettled in Kansas, Wapello County is unique among Iowa counties as it was rushed in a manner more readily associated with the settling of Oklahoma. However, despite efforts by Maj. John Beach, the area's second Indian agent, and the U.S. Dragoons to keep squatters and speculators out of the territory prior to the ratification of that treaty, one historian notes that "it would be taxing the credulity of our readers to assert that no violations of the spirit of the law were made by these pioneers . . ."

squatters
Indeed, one account reveals that James McMillin illegally staked

The photograph above shows the splendor of the current Wapello County Courthouse as it first appeared in 1894; above left, a close view of the damaged clock which was removed along with the tower in the 1950s; lower left, a worker is hoisted toward the statue of Chief Wapello.

Judge H. B. Hendershott, an attorney, moved to Ottumwa May 16, 1844. He was elected Judge of the District Court for the Third Judicial District in 1856.

Thomas Devin, a member of the Appanoose Rapids Company, served as an early justice of the peace. He also owned a store on Front Street in Ottumwa.

his 229-acre claim and then hid in Horse Thief Cave, near Cliffland, until the county was officially opened. The dragoons allegedly knew of McMillin's presence, but did not evict him.

The dragoons did force German immigrant John Groover off his illegal claim, near what is now Eldon, in 1842. Groover returned in 1843 and lived on his claim for three years before he died.

For those homesteaders who chose to abide by the law, establishing a claim by the light of the moon was not an easy task. According to Judge H. B. Hendershott, in an 1874 address to the Old Settlers' Association, "the work of locating and defining these claims, much of it being done in the night, was very inartistically done. Many of the lines were crooked, disjointed and encroached the one upon the other."

Hendershott said claims were often haphazardly marked by burning trees or bonfires by the leery settlers who then stood guard over their properties with guns and axes to ward off claim jumpers.

claim disputes

Disagreements were inevitable. Eventually, committees were established to address grievances and to render binding decisions as to the rightful ownership of disputed claims. Of course, if either party chose to ignore the authority of a committee, a fight ensued. One of the most famous claim disputes escalated into what is known as the Dahlonega War which is detailed in Chapter 4, Towns and Villages.

Infractions of a more sophisticated nature also occurred. The Appanoose Rapids Company, not by coincidence, claimed and platted the land that would become the county seat. Although unethical government surveyors provided the company with the foreknowledge that the governing body would be located at the geographical center of the new county, members of the speculation company still had to lobby extensively for that honor because of competition from the towns of Eddyville and Dahlonega. Louisville, the official name prior to the adoption of Ottumwa, was formally recognized as the county seat on Feb. 13, 1844.

first courthouse

A log cabin served as the courthouse until a new building was erected in 1846. The current courthouse, on Fourth and Court streets, was completed in 1894 (the looming clock tower and other ornamental chimneys were removed in 1950). Eventually,

fourteen civil townships were platted within Wapello County: Adams, Agency, Cass, Center, Columbia, Competine, Dahlonega, Green, Highland, Keokuk, Pleasant, Polk, Richland, and Washington.

life on the prairie

Pioneer life was difficult at best. In 1844, the Rev. Benjamin A. Spaulding, upon arriving from Massachusetts, recorded his initial impressions of pioneer life in the new territory in a letter to his fellow missionaries:

"It was literally a new country. Many of the settlers had not yet struck a furrow or erected a fence. All that reminded us that we were in a settled country, was the occasional sight of an incomplete cabin, in which we found families staying rather than living. They were not only destitute of conveniences, but were so open that the family could be seen about as well from the outside as by going in the door, or rather the hole that was left for

These Wapello County officials pictured above were on hand for the dedication of the new courthouse in 1894. Oliver Perry Bizer, right, was the chairman of the Wapello County Board of Supervisors at the time.

Early cabins, such as the one above, built by L. F. Newell near Agency in 1856, offered little more than shelter from the elements.

the door. How those families were to be comfortable, and how they were to be supplied with provisions during the inclement season, were questions that often occurred to us."

early cabins

Many of the initial settlers, poor and unskilled, quickly erected crude, makeshift cabins. Reminiscing in 1878, one unidentified historian offers a more detailed description of a typical first house:

"It is true, a claim cabin was a little more in the shape of a human habitation, made, as it was, of round logs light enough for two or three men to lay up, about fourteen feet square— perhaps a little larger or smaller— roofed with bark or clapboards, and sometimes with the sods of the prairie; and floored with puncheons (logs split in two, and the flat sides laid up), or with earth. For a fireplace, a wall of stone and earth— frequently the latter only, when stone was not convenient— was made in the

best practicable shape for the purpose, in an opening in one end of the building, extending onward, and planked on the outside by bolts of wood notched together to stay it . . .

"For doors and windows, the most simple contrivances that would serve the purposes were brought into requisition. The door was not always immediately provided with a shutter, and a blanket often did duty in guarding the entrance. But as soon as convenient, some boards were split and put together, hung upon hinges, and held shut by a wooden pin inserted in an auger hole. As a substitute for window glass, greased paper, pasted over sticks crossed in the shape of a sash, was sometimes used. This admitted the light and excluded the air, but of course lacked transparency.

"In regard to the furniture of such a cabin, of course it varied in proportion to the ingenuity of its occupants, unless it was where settlers brought with them their household supply, which, owing to the distance most of them had come, was very seldom. It was easy enough to improvise tables and chairs; the former could be made of split logs— and there were instances where the

door could be taken from its hinges and used at meals, after which it could be rehung— and the latter were designed after the three-legged stool pattern, or benches served their purpose. A bedstead was a very important item in the domestic comfort of the family, and this was the fashion of improvising them: A forked stake was driven into the ground diagonally from the corner of the room, and at a proper distance, upon which poles reaching from each wall were laid. The wall ends of the poles either rested in the openings between the logs or were driven into auger holes. Barks or boards were used as a substitute for cords. Upon this the tidy housewife spread her straw tick, and if she had a home-made feather bed, she piled it up in a luxurious mound and covered it with her whitest drapery. Some sheets hung behind it, for tapestry, added to the coziness of the resting place. This was generally called a 'prairie bedstead,' and by some the 'prairie rascal.'"

bread-stuff

As most homesteaders were barely self-subsistent during the first few years, obtaining and storing surplus food was imperative to their survival. In the beginning, many pioneers threshed and cleaned their own wheat for bread-stuff. However, the techniques were often so inefficient that the bread, laced with dirt and other residue, was often black.

Eventually commercial mills were established, but the settlers often had to endure long journeys by ox and cart across prairies that were void of roads, save the buffalo trails. In addition, depending on the season, they faced mud, flooding streams, and other obstacles of nature. If lucky enough to complete the trip, the early pioneer often had to then wait a week before his grain could be milled.

In 1905, Joseph W. Leinhauser, top left, makes apple cider while his wife, Marie Eleanor, top right, watches over a cauldron of apple butter on their farm near Agency. This picture of a barnyard made near Kirkville, circa 1900, shows the importance of horses to the early farmers in Wapello County. The animals provided transportation as well as the necessary power to plow the fields.

a farmer's diary

The diary of Dahlonega farmer Samuel Brown McClung offers some insight into the typical milling trip as well as other aspects of pioneer life:

"Tues. Dec. 28— Went to Skunk to mill—slept in mill overnight—returned home Wednesday. Saw elk, wolves, deer, squirrel and badger on way home." A man of few words, McClung also describes his winter chores in 1852: "Butchered; hauled wood; husked corn; hauled fodder; hauled water; cut rails." According to later entries, the farmer's round trip from near Dahlonega to the mill at Bonaparte in Van Buren County took approximately six days in March of 1853.

As these early pioneers began to provide for their basic survival needs in the new county, they quickly turned their attention to the fertile Iowa land and the plow.

Descendants of Samuel Brown McClung found life on the farm somewhat easier with the help of modern technology. Left, members of the Fred McClung (Samuel's son) family operate their combine— reportedly the first in Wapello County, circa 1920s. The McClung Century Farm is located in Pleasant Township. Fred McClung served as Wapello County supervisor from 1921 to 1926 and 1930 to 1935.

Neighbors came from near and far to help John
Sylvester raise a barn on his farm just south of the
former town of Competine, in Competine Township, circa 1900.

A Wapello County farmer uses a team of horses to pull a load of corn stalks on his farm near Kirkville at the turn of the century.

agriculture

althoughwhite settlers didn't officially arrive in Wapello County until 1843, ground was broken for the first farm five years earlier in 1838. The treaty of 1837— the Second Black Hawk Purchase— stipulated that a model farm would be established to teach the Sac and Fox tribes how to grow wheat and corn. Three farms were established near each of the three villages located just below and opposite of Ottumwa. The farms were financed through the annuities awarded to the Native Americans for the sale of their land.

According to Maj. John Beach, the farms failed because the Sac and Fox, who hunted for survival, looked upon manual labor with disdain. In addition, Beach writes, the farms were devised by opportunists for "plundering the savages and fastening upon them [a] host of vampires and leeches, schemes causing the outlay of many thousands of dollars of the money granted to these Indians for their lands, from which, it is safe to say that they never derived the slightest benefit."

census reports and statistics

By 1850, the non-Indian population of Wapello County had surged to 8,479 and continued to grow in leaps and bounds. Census reports indicate that by 1875 the population reached 23,855. Ottumwa was by far the biggest town boasting 7,501 residents and 1,028 families. Of course most of the county's residents were engaged in farming and other related endeavors.

Although Iowa was the first state born of the Louisiana Purchase to outlaw slavery, only 318 African-Americans lived in Wapello County by 1875. Julian Oscar Winston and his wife, Lucy, were among the first African-American farmers. They arrived from Virginia in 1906 and purchased a dairy farm south of Ottumwa two years later.

Statistics from 1874 show that 135,173 acres of Wapello County were under cultivation. Spring wheat and oats were the primary crops followed by winter wheat and Indian corn. Farm products were valued at an estimated $1.4 million.

In 1887 William and Mary Bonnett bought this farm south of Farson in Competine Township. The farm was complete with a wooden windmill, circa 1915.

Ottumwa was the home of several wholesalers of dairy products in the late 1800s, but a number of small dairies also operated in the county. Above, young Charles Thorne greets Berniece Leighton who is seated in a truck owned by Charles E. Mast Dairies, circa 1932.

dairies, pork and wool

As early as 1878, one unidentified historian predicted that Wapello County was destined to become one of the most profitable dairy regions, as well as the foremost producer of hogs and sheep, in the state. He writes: "The county is new, and men have not determined what branches of industry to pursue; but nature will settle that question for them and bear us out in our assertions. The historian who takes up our work 50 years from today will refer to this prediction, and admit that it was based on solid calculation."

Those predictions were realized before fifty years had passed. According to the *Ottumwa Courier Annual Trade Edition* of 1893, Ottumwa was home to the "Butter King of the West"— Samuel Lilburn. Lilburn owned and operated Samuel Lilburn & Co., located at Second and Green Streets, prior to his death in 1887. In 1890, the thriving company shipped 2 million pounds of butter across the United States. In the same year, the wholesaler transported 2 million dozen eggs. Baker Bros. Butter & Egg Shippers, founded in 1878, provided a similar service.

John Morrell & Company moved its entire U.S. operation to Ottumwa in 1878. In the foreground of this photograph, circa 1899, is the former area known as Wigglesville. Many meat packers there lived until the company bought the land in the 1940s.

The decision by John Morrell & Company to move its entire U.S. operation to Ottumwa in 1878 underscored the strength of the swine market in Wapello County. The defunct Mitchell-Ladd packing plant, located on the north side of the Des Moines River near Vine Street, became the company's first home.

By 1892, the Ottumwa packing house could process 3,000 hogs daily. Smaller meat packing houses existed in Eddyville and Dahlonega prior to the arrival of Morrell's.

As early as 1874, the sheep flock numbered 18,790 and the wool clip was 62, 225 pounds.

farm organizations and county fairs

Several farm organizations emerged in the early days. A sampling includes the Wapello County Agricultural Society, organized January 24, 1852, and the Wapello County Farmers' Institute, which first met in 1905 to introduce and debate new farming techniques. The Wapello County Farm Bureau dates back to 1917.

The first county fair, organized in 1852 by the Wapello County Agricultural Society, drew at least 2,000 persons. The Wapello County Fair and Exposition opened in 1882. In 1890, representatives from Wapello, Jefferson, Davis, and Van Buren counties met to organize the Eldon Big Four District Agricultural Association and The Eldon Big 4 Fair. That event was discontinued in 1917. The current Wapello County Fair was first held in 1922. The Wapello County 4-H Program for boys began in 1918 followed by the girls' chapter in the mid-1920s.

the great depression

Unfortunately, the next important period affecting agriculture in Wapello County was the Great Depression. Although Wapello County fared better than some regions of the country in the late 1920s and most of the 1930s, it certainly experienced its share of hard times. By 1932, corn prices had plummeted to 10 cents a bushel and many corn fields were decimated by grasshopper and chinch bug infestations.

Farm census reports for 1934 show that in Wapello County the acreage of land on which all crops failed totaled 17,189 compared to 1,489 in 1929, the year of the stock market crash. The average value per acre dropped to $50.12 in 1934 from $98.90 in 1929. Farm foreclosures became the lamentable norm.

Lyle Henry's Chester White hog won the grand champion prize at the 1917 county fair. Henry lived in Competine Township.

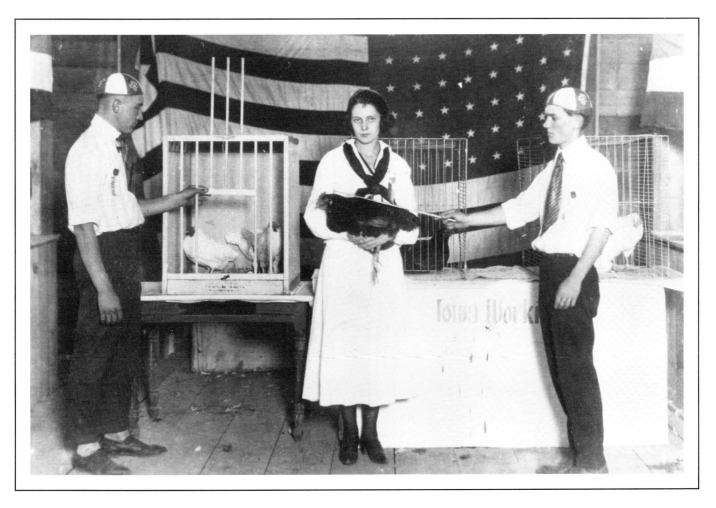

Ottumwa's Herman Swanson, right, traveled to the 1922 State Fair in Des Moines to judge the poultry contest. The young woman is Martha Pepper.

This photograph of a threshing rig in Highland Township, circa 1912, shows how many men were required to operate the cumbersome machine. The men are, left to right, Earl Birkinbine, Otto Krusemark, Benny Rooker and Henry Knuth. The two men on the far left are not identified. The rig was owned by Rooker and Knuth.

Above, members of the I. E. Peck family working a field in south Ottumwa near what is now the John Deere Ottumwa Works, circa 1908.

By 1939, threshing rigs were much easier to operate. Pictured are members of the Roy Harter family on their farm north of Ottumwa.

A Richland Township farmer, right, cutting corn by hand, circa 1900.

On the opposite page, top left, Everett Garber and Willis Breon oil a windmill on a farm north of Ottumwa, circa 1935; top right George, Lafe and Maggie Kinder pose in front of a sorghum mill with their dog, Spot, circa 1939; and, bottom right, harvesting Sudan grass near the old Jim Jordan place southeast of Eldon are, left to right, Newt Breckenridge, Frank Carlos, Henry Cudworth and Madeline Spilman, circa 1922.

The two farmers below use a homemade winch and pulley system to stack a mound of hay on a farm in Richland Township near Kirkville, circa 1900.

Lowell Sedore of Keokuk Township, south of Ottumwa, uses a John Deere baler to compress and bind the hay into uniform bales, circa 1939.

William B. Bonnifield, right, and farm hand, Carl Wymore, at a sale barn located in the 300 block of West Second Street in Ottumwa, circa 1915.

A rare view of Ottumwa from East Main Street be-
fore the city avenues were paved, circa 1880.

towns
and villages

defiance, Opposition, Fairplay— the implied meanings of those words seem almost contradictory considering that they were also the names of early settlements or villages that were abandoned while Wapello County was still in its infancy.

More than 50 such villages once dotted the countryside, according to articles found in the *Annals of Iowa* (see map). Of course, most were not incorporated towns, but apparently a few were deemed large enough to warrant a post office, or to at least be considered a mail drop. Some, like Amador, located near Blakesburg in the mid-1850s, were comprised of nothing more than a general store.

early settlements

Many of those earliest settlements were nestled along the Des Moines River between Ottumwa and Eddyville. Some were on the stagecoach line or, later, next to the railroad tracks. Others

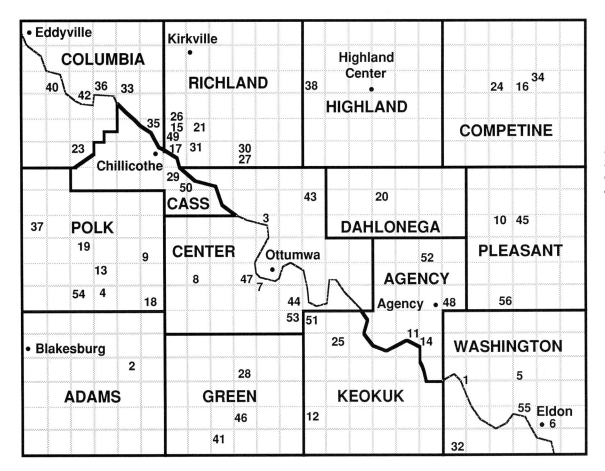

The map contains the following labels:

• Eddyville

COLUMBIA
40 42 36 33

Kirkville
•

RICHLAND

Highland
Center
•
HIGHLAND
38

24 16 34

COMPETINE

35

26
15 21
49
23
17 31
Chillicothe

30
27

29
50
CASS

43

20

This map shows
Wapello County be-
fore the Des Moines
River was straight-
ened near Ottumwa
after the 1947 flood.

37 POLK
19
9
13
54 4
18

3

CENTER
8   47
7

Ottumwa
•

DAHLONEGA

52
AGENCY

Agency • 48

10 45

PLEASANT

56

44
53 51

• Blakesburg
2

28

ADAMS   GREEN
46
41

25

KEOKUK
12

11
14

1
32

WASHINGTON
5

55 Eldon
• 6

abandoned towns and hamlets in wapello county

In the past 149 years there have been at least 64 towns or hamlets in Wapello County. The approximate locations of the following abandoned towns, villages and post office locations were determined from information presented in early editions of the *Annals of Iowa*:

1.) Alpine: Post office, 1860 to 1872, section 18, Washington Township.

2.) Amador: Section 14, Adams Township.

3.) Amsterdam: In 1843, center of section 14, Center Township, about two miles northwest of Ottumwa's business section.

4.) Appanoose: Post office, 1890 and 1891, near Willard, Polk Township.

5.) Ashland: Section 9, Washington Township, about three miles north of Eldon. Post office, 1844 to 1880.

6.) Ashland Crossing: Name first given the place that later became Williamsburg and, finally, Eldon.

7.) Ayersville: In 1843, section 26, Center Township. Appears to have been later called Port Richmond.

8.) Bear Creek: Station on Chicago, Minneapolis & St. Paul Railroad, about four miles west of Ottumwa. Post office, 1900 to 1914.

9.) Bidwell: Post office, 1888 to 1913 and 1915 to 1921, section 24, Polk Township, about five miles from Ottumwa on Milwaukee Railroad.

10.) Bladensburg: Village, section 16, Pleasant Township. Post office, 1855 to 1916.

11.) Bryson: Post office, 1872, at or near former railroad station of Cliffland, Agency Township.

12.) Burton: Station on Wabash Railroad, about eight miles south of Ottumwa, western part of Keokuk Township.

13.) Christianburg: Section 27, Polk Township. Post office, 1859 to 1872.

14.) Cliffland: Post office at Keokuk & Des Moines Valley Railroad station, 1872 to 1875, section 11, Agency Township.

15.) Columbia: Post office, 1846 to 1849. Name changed to Fountain Spring in 1849.

16.) Competine: Post office, section 15, Competine Township, 1851 to 1903. Formerly Marysville.

17.) Comstock: Kirkville Station. Comstock was the name of post office, 1861 to 1877.

18.) Coopersville: Post office, 1867 to 1875, center of section 26, Polk Township.

19.) Cynthiann: Post office, 1850 to 1852, near center of Polk Township.

20.) Dahlonega: Five miles northeast of Ottumwa, section 9, Dahlonega Township. Post office, 1844 to 1907.

21.) Defiance: In 1843, common corners of sections 20, 21, 28 and 29, Richland Township, about two miles northeast of Kirkville Station.

22.) Des Moines City: Listed as post office in Wapello County, 1851 to 1853. However, early maps show it to have been in Mahaska County.

23.) Dudley: Post office, 1870 to 1939, section 33, Columbia Township, on Chicago, Burlington & Quincy Railroad.

24.) Farson: Post office, 1903 to 1957, sections 16 and 17, Competine Township. Moved from Competine.

25.) Fairplay: In 1843, post office, south half of section 8, Keokuk Township.

26.) Fountain Spring: Post office, 1849 to 1873, formerly Columbia.

27.) Godfrey: Richland Township, at or near Keb. Post office, 1872 to 1874.

28.) Green: Slightly north of center, Green Township. Post office, 1851 to 1859.

29.) Happy Hollow: Post office, 1870 to 1877, near Shock's Station.

30.) Keb: Post office, section 34, Richland Township, 1891 to 1905.

31.) Kirkville Station: Post office, 1861 to 1877, section 30, Richland Township.

32.) Laddsdale: Post office, 1880 to about 1919, section 31, Washington Township.

33.) Marion: In 1843, town and post office, sections 14 and 15, Columbia Township, north bank of the Des Moines River.

34.) Marysville: Renamed Competine (see Competine).

35.) Mechanicsburg: In 1843, sections 24 and 25, Columbia Township, north bank of the Des Moines River.

36.) Midlothian: In 1843, a town in section 15, Columbia Township, north bank of the Des Moines River.

37.) Munterville: Hamlet and post office, 1875 to 1905, section 17, Polk Township.

38.) Morton: Post office, 1878 and 1879, possibly in west part of Highland Township.

39.) Nanisee: Listed as a Wapello County post office, 1854 and 1855. Location not indicated in existing records.

40.) Opposition: In 1843, town in south part of section 8, north part of section 17, Columbia Township, north side of the Des Moines River.

41.) Ormanville: Town and post office, 1869 to 1903, section 13, Green Township.

42.) Palestine: Near center of Columbia Township, north side of the Des Moines River, some four miles southeast of Eddyville, according to an 1857 map.

43.) Phillips: Formerly Rutledge, station on the Milwaukee Railroad, three miles north of Ottumwa.

44.) Pickwick: Former name of south Ottumwa.

45.) Pleasant Lane: Post office, 1854 and 1855, at or near village of Bladensburg.

46.) Point Isabel: Post office, 1851 to 1868, section 27, Green Township.

47.) Port Richmond: Section 27, Center Township, about one mile south of Pickwick. Post office, 1858 to 1875.

48.) Sac and Fox Agency: Name of post office, 1844 to 1849. Later became Agency City, then Agency.

49.) Sailorville: In 1843, sections 19 and 30, Richland Township, about one mile north of Kirkville Station.

50.) Shock's Station: Station on the Chicago, Burlington & Quincy Railroad, section 5, Cass Township, two miles southeast of Chillicothe, south side of the Des Moines River.

51.) Sickles: Station on the Wabash Railroad, about three miles south of Ottumwa, according to an 1887 map.

52.) Tunis: Post office, about two miles north of Agency, 1897 to 1900.

53.) Village: Post office southeast of Ottumwa, south side of the Des Moines River, 1847 to 1850.

54.) Willard: Station on Chicago, Minneapolis & St. Paul Railroad, section 33, Polk Township. Post office, 1890 to 1906.

55.) Willamsburg: Name of post office, 1868 to 1871. Town's name changed to Eldon in 1870.

56.) Yampa: Post office, 1899 and 1900, south part of Pleasant Township, according to a 1900 map.

were created by the various coal mining interests that operated in the county from the late 1800s to the 1920s.

Villages noted by surveyor William Vandever in 1843—the same year the county was opened to homesteaders— were Amsterdam, located two miles northwest of Ottumwa; Ayersville, two miles southwest of Ottumwa and later called Port Richmond; Defiance, about four miles south of Kirkville; Fairplay, three miles southeast of Ottumwa; Marion, four miles southeast of Eddyville; Mechanicsburg, one mile north of Chillicothe on the north side of the Des Moines River; Midlothian, three miles southeast of Eddyville; Opposition, two miles south of Eddyville on the south side of the Des Moines River; and Sailorville, about four miles south of Kirkville. Available history texts do not indicate why the above settlements failed.

dahlonega and ashland

Dahlonega, located five miles northeast of Ottumwa, and Ashland, almost three miles north of Eldon, were once prosperous towns on the stagecoach line.

Dahlonega, originally known as Shellbark, was a bustling town in 1860 with a population of about 300.

Dahlonega, originally called Shellbark, has a rich history. Most county residents are familiar with the oft-told story of the Dahlonega War that pitted James Woody against Martin Koontz, presumedly in 1843. As the story is told, Woody tried to repossess a claim that he sold to Koontz for $200 in gold. The Claims Committee favored Koontz's position, but Woody refused to abide by the ruling. Both men mustered their friends into small armies and a fight ensued. Thomas Crawford, fighting on Woody's behalf, was killed.

As Wapello County had not been formally organized, Jefferson County Deputy Sheriff Woolard attempted to arrest the leaders of Koontz's party for the murder. Instead, they captured Woolard. He was allowed to return home the following morning, but not until he had been paraded around the public square. Koontz kept the claim.

Dahlonega also competed with Ottumwa for the county seat, but lost by one vote. According to Ottumwa resident Ben Mirgon, his uncle, Lewis Clapp, of Dahlonega, cast a critical nay vote because he feared that people would steal apples from

Julia Clapp, pictured above in 1916, was a school teacher and the wife of Lewis Clapp who, in 1844, voted against Dahlonega becoming the county seat. Pictured below are students of the Dahlonega School, circa 1920.

Students still attending Ashland School in the early 1900s were, front row, left to right, Carmen Miller, Hannibel Springer, Glen Acton, Dorothy Munroe, Glen Cash, Earl Cash, Harry Foster, Troy (last name unknown), Leo (last name unknown), (first name unknown) Drake, (first name unknown) Drake, Neva Acton; middle row, left to right, George Black, Marion Springer, Ira Jameson, Emmett Jameson, and Glenn Drake. Pictured in the back row, left to right, are Lena Stewart (teacher), Freda Warren, Eva Black, Frank Beall, Will Acton, unknown, Wayne Warren, Everett Marsh, Grace Warren, Clara Jameson, and Nita Rouke (teacher).

his orchard if the town's population increased. Ottumwa, of course, became the county seat in 1844.

Ashland's history began with the establishment of the stagecoach line and ended with the arrival of the railroads. Businessman Thomas Ping was instrumental in building the town on land that he owned along the old Indian trail, or the eventual State Road. Ping opened the first bank and Peter Ballingall, of Ottumwa fame, constructed the town's first hotel, Ashland House. Other businesses in Ashland included four stores, a brick plant and a sawmill. Ashland Seminary was in operation from 1854 to 1858. Railroads proved to be the death of Ashland when they bypassed the town in favor of Eldon, formerly known as Ashland Crossing. When the post office closed in 1880, Ashland was destined to be buried by the plow.

tunis and yampa

Two short-lived towns, Tunis and Yampa, were abandoned in 1900.

Tunis, located one-half mile north of Agency on what is

now the Hedrick-Agency Highway, served as a station on the "Peavine" railroad beginning in 1892. The station building also housed a general store and a post office. Additional businesses included a mill and a feed store. The railroad that operated between Ottumwa and Ft. Madison was abandoned in 1900 and the mail went to Yampa.

Located one-half mile north of the intersection of Highways 34 and 89 (The Eldon Y) near Honey Creek, Yampa survived about one month longer than Tunis. Store proprietor Clell Farley owned the only building that existed in the town. Temple School was also located near Yampa.

coal mining towns

Laddsdale, Bidwell and Keb were among a number of towns created in the county by the coal mining industry of the late 1800s. Typical of company towns of that era, they disappeared when the mines were abandoned.

Laddsdale was located southwest of Eldon near the Davis County line. Although the post office wasn't established until

The people below were photographed while visiting the underground mule stables at Laddsdale, circa 1910. Mules were used to haul coal from the mines.

This building reportedly housed the company store near the Keb coal mine in Richland Township, circa 1905.

The Bidwell Coal Company employed up to 150 men until tho mino, locatod fivo miloc woot of Ottumwa, closed in the early 1920s.

1880, the Southwest Coal & Mining Company operated a slope mine there as early as 1872. Ten years later, the Eldon Coal & Mining Company, with W. R. Daum of Ottumwa as its president, took over the business. Several other companies also mined coal there until 1918.

Laddsdale had a company store as well as two schools and two hotels— one each in Wapello and Davis counties. Of course, the mining company owned the store and workers risked being fired if they tried to buy groceries elsewhere. Despite that fear, residents reportedly patronized a Floris grocer who sold his goods in Laddsdale under the cover of night. Although an exact date is not given, the miners apparently formed a union around 1901 and immediately petitioned the company to build a public road through the town that extended through both counties. Prior to that, the company had resisted building an accessible road through Laddsdale. By 1918, all coal mining operations had ceased.

Before the arrival of the Homer Harris Coal Company in 1913, Bidwell was nothing more than a cluster of four houses located five miles southwest of Ottumwa along the Milwaukee Railroad line. Ten years after the discovery of a profitable coal mine, the town grew to include 100 houses, two schools, a roller skating rink and a baseball field. Unlike most company towns, there were two stores in Bidwell— only one was owned by the miners' employer. The Bidwell Coal Company eventually took over the operation and employed up to 150 men until the mine closed in the early 1920s.

Keb, founded in 1891, was located in Richland Township five miles north of Ottumwa. A prosperous mining operation amid some of the richest coal deposits in the state, the town's population peaked at just more than 300. Keb's last hurrah came at the 1904 Labor Day celebration which, according to the Ottumwa *Daily Courier*, was the largest in the town's history. The mine closed in 1905.

Other abandoned mines in the county were either at or near the towns of Alpine, Dahlonega, Dudley, Eddyville, Godfrey, Happy Hollow, Kirkville, Ormanville, Ottumwa, Phillips and Willard.

a town by any other name

Over the years, several past and present Wapello County towns have been known by different names. Jordan City, Williamsburg and Ashland Crossing all refer to the same town— Eldon. Ottumwa was originally called Louisville, the name of the first

Agency's Main Street was a dirt road lined with trees before the turn of the century.

Will Reynolds, left, owned and operated the Agency Roller Mills, circa 1900.

post office established there in 1843.

Marysville became Competine upon the discovery that another Iowa town had the same name. To avoid the same confusion, Blakesburg reassumed its current name after it was inexplicably changed to Cleveland for two years in the late 1800s. Columbia, founded in 1846, became Fountain Spring in 1849. It was abandoned in 1873. Agency used to be Agency City and, before that, the Sac and Fox Indian Agency.

central addition, wigglesville and smoky row

Within the town of Ottumwa, some areas or neighborhoods assumed an identity of their own. Greater Ottumwa Park used to be known as Central Addition. Wigglesville once stood just east of Morrell's meat packing plant (see Chapter 3, Agriculture). Smoky Row, an impoverished section of town, was located along Mill Street in Ottumwa's east end.

Central Addition, developed in the late 1800s by the Ottumwa Land Company, was touted as an ideal place to reside. Unfortunately, it was also on the river's flood plain. The almost annual flooding, beginning in 1893, forced many residents to move to higher ground. Still, many poor families remained there for more than 50 years. The 1947 flood all but obliterated the area.

Many Wigglesville residents were employed by Morrell's, which purchased most of their properties in the 1940s to build a parking lot. Wigglesville's most noted resident was Ralph O'Dell. The Ottumwa High School football star earned all-state honors in 1933 and 1934.

Smoky Row had a notorious reputation as the home of tough bars and brothels. Ottumwa artist David Edstrom lived there as a child and wrote about the experience in his 1937 autobiography, *The Testament of Caliban*. Edstrom sculpted the bust of Abraham Lincoln that is displayed in the Wapello County Historical Museum.

Edward O'Dell, left, owned and operated the O'Dell's Grocery in Wigglesville from 1905 to 1915. To O'Dell's right are Stella Hatfield Walker and Eva O'Dell Bigg. The property was sold to Morrell's in 1940.

surviving towns and villages

By the mid-1940s only a handful of towns and villages existed in Wapello County: Agency, Bladensburg, Blakesburg, Chillicothe, Eddyville, Eldon, Farson, Highland Center, Kirkville and Ottumwa. The following are synopses of their early histories:

Agency is the legacy of the Sac and Fox Indian Agency established in 1838 by Gen. Joseph Street. The agency was located just southeast of the town near Chief Wapello Memorial Park.

Gen. Street's son-in-law, Capt. George Wilson, created the

An aerial view of Bladensburg. Located in Pleasant Township, the village was settled in 1853.

The Hardy House, a hotel located in Blakesburg, was owned and operated by Frank and Metilda Hardy. The building was razed prior to 1920.

Charles Peterson owned and operated the C. W. Peterson & Co. store in Chillicothe, circa 1901. Peterson also served a stint as the town's postmaster.

first plat of Agency City in 1843. Agency's Main Street— U. S. Highway 34— once served as a race course for Chief Keokuk's braves, according to one history text.

Bladensburg, although platted in 1853, was never incorporated. In addition, according to articles in the *Annals of Iowa*, the village might have been known as Pleasant Lane in 1854. The first post office bearing Bladensburg's name dates back to 1855; it closed in 1916.

Located in the center of Pleasant Township, the village once had a population of 200 and supported three stores, two blacksmith shops, three churches, a sawmill, flour mill, two saloons, an I.O.O.F. lodge and a school, according to Ottumwa resident Paul Kesselring.

Blakesburg is the namesake of Theophilus Blake, who laid out the town in 1850 or 1852, depending on the source. Located in Adams Township, its population reached 500 by 1856.

By 1860, almost half of the residents moved away because the railroads had bypassed the town. The town was revived when the Chicago, Milwaukee and St. Paul Railroad arrived on New Year's Eve, 1887. Blakesburg was incorporated in 1900.

Past businesses of note include the Hardy House hotel, the Fritz Opera House, and Fritz Hardware. The two banks that operated in the town, the Blakesburg Savings Bank and People's Savings Bank, folded during the Great Depression of the 1930s.

Eight miles west of Ottumwa is the town of Chillicothe. Originally a station on the Chicago, Burlington & Quincy Railroad, a plat was filed in 1849, the same year the post office opened. The town was incorporated in 1881. In 1910, the residents numbered 181. Six years later the population increased slightly to 190.

Jabish P. Eddy established a trading post at the present site of Eddyville in 1840. He platted the town in 1843 after receiving a government land grant of 640 acres. Fourteen years later the town was incorporated.

In the early 1850s, Eddyville was regarded as the starting point of the Oregon Trail. In 1852, pioneer and author Ezra Meeker reportedly arrived in Eddyville with his wife and son to begin the five-month journey to Oregon.

The following passage is an excerpt from the *Revised Ordinances, City of Eldon, 1899*: "The site which is now occupied by our beautiful and busy little city of about two thousand population, was, 35 years ago, a forest and brush covered hillside; the home of Black Hawk and his tribe of Sac and Fox Indians."

Considering its size, Eldon's contribution to local history

The above photograph shows downtown Eddyville, circa 1920.

is quite significant. It is the site of the Gothic House made famous by artist Grant Wood; the Bearing Tree, used by surveyors in 1846 to plot the state's borders; and the former Jordan house, with its drive-in basement designed to accommodate stagecoaches. A railroad boom town, Eldon was incorporated in 1872.

The Chicago, Milwaukee & St. Paul Railway literally created the town of Farson in Competine Township. Located 15 miles northeast of Ottumwa, a railroad camp was established at Farson in 1902. That same year a storm leveled every building, save a stable. The first trains arrived in 1903. In creating Farson, the railroad company all but razed the nearby town of Competine.

Highland Center, a former stop on the stagecoach line between Dahlonega and Hedrick, was actually located just more than a mile northeast of its present location. When the Chicago, Milwaukee & St. Paul Railway arrived in 1882, the town was

The Jordan house, top left, formerly located just south of Eldon, served as a unique stop on the stagecoach route because the coach and horses could actually park in its basement. In addition, owner James Jordan buried his friend Chief Black Hawk near the structure in 1838. The house was razed in 1964. Iowa artist Grant Wood used the house on the top right as the backdrop for his famous 1930 painting, American Gothic. The house is still standing in Eldon. The bottom photograph provides a view from Fourth and Main Street in Eldon, circa 1920.

Barber Ben Byron Mirgon, far left, opposite page, operated one of the few businesses to exist in Highland Center, circa 1909. Left, the Highland Center Depot, built in 1882, was dismantled in 1937.

Farson, bottom, opposite page, as seen from the grain elevator near the railroad tracks, circa 1917.

Rural mail carrier Will Graham, right, at the Kirkville Post Office prior to the turn of the century.

moved closer to the tracks.

A tragic train wreck in 1892 killed four passengers when a south-bound freight train plowed into the caboose of another train that had stopped at Highland Center to unload its freight. The depot was sold in 1937.

Kirkville lies in Richland Township, one of the first townships organized in the county in 1844. The town is named for John Kirkpatrick who contracted to have the town platted in 1848. The first house was built there in 1853 and by 1890, thanks to coal mining in the area, the population had reached 714. The population declined throughout the early 1900s. By 1925 only 226 residents remained.

Ottumwa, the county seat, was the brainchild of the Appanoose Rapids Company. Armed with the secret that the county seat would be located at the geographical center of the county, as well as the results of an illegal survey conducted by John Arrowsmith prior to the May 1, 1843 opening of the county, members of the speculation company claimed the land near the Appanoose Rapids of the Des Moines River.

The first house was built in Ottumwa during 1843. One year later, the town consisted of nine log cabins, one framed house, a store and a small hotel known as the Ottumwa House. The town was incorporated in 1851. Ottumwa quickly established itself as the county's industrial and transportation center in the late 1800s.

The above scenes from Ottumwa include, clockwise from the top, a pan-
oramic view of the city looking northeast toward Adams School or the present
location of Ottumwa High School, circa 1880; the construction of the federal
building, circa 1912, which first housed the post office and, eventually, Ottumwa City Hall in 1964; the post office located at the corner of Third and
Court streets (where Ottumwa City Hall now stands), circa 1890; and the
former city hall, built in 1873, on Market Street, circa 1950.

The Hoffman Building fire in downtown Ottumwa on Easter morning, March 24, 1940.

A crowd gathers at Ottumwa Fire Station No. 1, circa 1903.

Capt. John Shockley and his unidentified driver leaving the South Ottumwa Fire Station located at Ransom and Church streets, circa 1912.

A new aerial ladder truck and a fire hose truck at Ottumwa Fire Station No. 1, circa 1914.

Members of the Ottumwa Police Department in 1899 were (first name un-known) Cobble, Chief H. C. Williams, Mayor T. J. Phillips (front, third from left), Police Judge Charles Hall (front, fourth from left), Captain John Gray, Andy Pitts, Levi Noaha, William Maloney, C. Myers, G. Pansan, Frank Schwartz, Charles Peterson, John Niemeyer, and Lawrence Kent. The above names were not provided in a sequence that reflects the position of each individual in the photograph. In addition, six names are missing.

Facing the camera are Ottumwa policemen L. L. Lightner, W. Criswell, and J. W. Gray, circa 1915. The officers appear to be standing on the south side of the Market Street Bridge.

Ottumwa police officer Oscar Hendricks, circa 1915.

An aerial view of the Des Moines River, near Ottumwa, during the 1947 flood.

the river

eight days after Wapello County was opened to settlers in 1843, the steamer *Ione*— a conflicting report claims the boat was called the *Agatha*— transported federal troops from Garrison Rock to Raccoon Fork, or what is now the city of Des Moines. That inaugural trip, made in the seasonally high waters, fueled speculation that the Des Moines River could be navigated by Mississippi River steamboats.

early attempts to improve the river

Three years later, a federal land grant was issued to the Territory of Iowa to encourage the improvement of the Des Moines River for navigational purposes. The grant reserved a five mile strip of land, in alternate sections of available public lands, on each side of the Des Moines River from its mouth to the Raccoon Fork. The act also prompted the establishment of a public utility— sometimes referred to as the Des Moines River Improvement Company— to build dams and locks on the river.

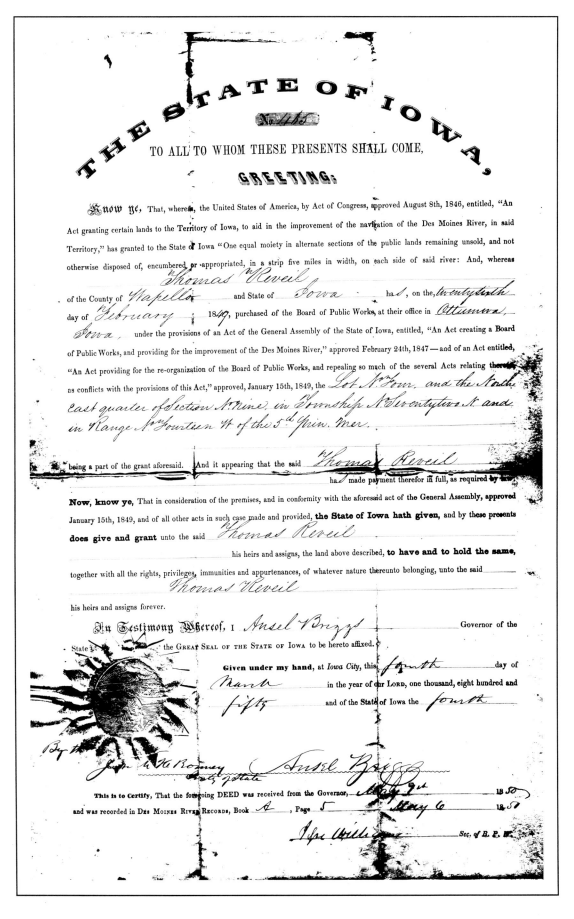

In 1849, Wapello County resident Thomas Reveal purchased a section of land, between Ottumwa and Eddyville, made available through a federal land grant designed to encourage the improvement of the Des Moines River for navigational purposes. To the left is the deed issued to Reveal by Iowa Gov. Ansel Briggs.

Almost immediately a political dispute emerged as to whether the grant included, what was then, the unexplored upper valley of the river. That dissension was exacerbated by the inflated reports of speculators regarding the feasibility of the project.

At least one Wapello County resident bought land under the guidelines of the federal grant. Thomas Reveal purchased a section of land along the river between Ottumwa and Eddyville in 1849. One year later, he and his wife, Elizabeth, deeded a parcel of the land to Center Township's School District Number Three. It eventually became the site of Reveal School.

river project abandoned

During the 1850s, the state project (Iowa was granted statehood Dec. 28, 1846) was dealt death blows by unscrupulous developers and the continued political squabbling. Finally, with the increased excitement surrounding the building of railroads, the utility was formally disbanded in 1860. An occasional steamboat might be spotted on the river in Wapello County between Ot-

Reveal School, below, was built after Thomas and Elizabeth Reveal deeded a parcel of land to School District Number Three, Center Township of Wapello County in 1850. The Reveals were paid one dollar for the property. The land was originally purchased from the state in conjunction with the ill-fated river improvement plan.

A small steamer on the Des Moines River, circa 1896.

Below, a mountain of sand dredged from the Des Moines River at Eddyville, circa 1920.

The steamboat above belonged to the Eddyville Sand Company, circa 1915.

tumwa and Keosauqua in Van Buren County, but such a sighting was rare by 1862.

Historian Charles Negus, writing in an early edition of the *Annals of Iowa*, offers this epitaph for the project:

"This was a most magnificent grant, embracing some of the best lands in the [s]tate; and if the proceeds had been judiciously and properly expended, would have made a great thoroughfare for steamboats, besides affording an immense water-power for driving machinery. But, through the incompetency of managing the means, and the intrigues of designing men, the whole of the lands below the Raccoon Fork, and a large quantity above, were disposed of, and very little practical good accomplished toward the navigation of the river."

Despite Negus' argument, many historians doubt that the river could have ever been made navigable for the larger steamboats.

river projects in wapello county

If early records are correct, the Wapello County Commissioners appeared to be one step ahead of the territorial and federal governments. In July of 1845, county officials authorized Henry Smith & Co. to build a dam at Ashland Crossing, or what is now the town of Eldon. Evidently, the project was abandoned during the same year. A stone house built for the lock tender was never occupied.

Officials also licensed several ferries in the county. The first was granted to J. P. Eddy on May 10, 1844. Eddy established the ferry at Eddyville. The commissioners allowed him to charge the following prices: footman— 6 1/2 cents, man and horse— 18 3/4 cents, two horses and wagon— 37 1/2 cents, four horses and wagon— 50 cents, cattle— 4 cents, and hogs— 2 cents.

A second license was approved during the same year for the Appanoose Rapids Company with the provisions that the ferry be free of charge and that half of the building and maintenance expenses be paid by the company. Although difficult to document beyond a reasonable doubt, more than likely this ferry operated at the approximate location of the present Market Street Bridge in Ottumwa. Anderson Cox was allowed to operate another ferry one and one-fourth miles above Ottumwa. The Overman Ferry, near the former Port Richmond, or what is now the intersection of Richmond and Ferry streets, transported passengers to and from old Central Addition. The inevitable construction of bridges, such as the Eddyville Toll Bridge during the

Left, the Market Street Bridge after a section was washed away by high waters, circa 1893.

On the opposite page is another view of the Market Street Bridge, built in 1892, that connects Market Street with Church Street on the south side of Ottumwa, circa 1896.

The original Ottumwa Water Works building, circa 1880.

late 1850s, washed the ferries into obsolescence.

the ottumwa water-power company

The next attempt to tap the resources of the Des Moines River occurred in 1875 with the establishment of the Ottumwa Water-Power Company. The company contracted with the firm of D. B. Sears & Son to construct two dams extending across the river from Turkey Island. Floods and high waters destroyed the early structures and the contractor abandoned the project in 1877. The company sued D. B. Sears & Son, but the results of the litigation cannot be found in available history texts.

That same year, the company was reorganized as the Ottumwa Water Works and it successfully entered into a 25-year contract with engineer S. L. Wiley of Massachusetts.

According to a 1914 account by county historian Harrison Waterman, the company refused to offer its services when requested by south Ottumwa officials. Shortly thereafter, indig-

The present hydro-electric plant— the second in Ottumwa— was built in 1930. The first structure was built in 1914 and was located just west of the above plant.

nant residents threatened to form the South Ottumwa Water Company. Wiley, who had been elected president of the Ottumwa Water Works, quickly conceded and offered to lay pipes across the river if the south Ottumwa residents abandoned their idea of forming a competing enterprise.

The current location of the Ottumwa Water Works on South Wapello Street was established in 1903 by the Public Water Company. In 1910, the facility became city property.

A new complex was proposed that eventually led to the construction of the hydro-electric plant and a powerhouse on the river, just above the Market Street Bridge, in 1914. The present hydro plant, located just down the river from the original, was built in 1930.

water recreation
Power and city water were not the only offerings of the Des Moines River. Water recreation and sports— especially rowing

Left, Opal Cook, first woman from the right, enjoys a summer swim with friends at the Ottumwa boat house, circa 1915. Below, the Ottumwa Oarsmen club poses on the steps of the boat house, circa 1900.

Former Ottumwa Courier Publisher James F. Powell, left, shows his rowing form, circa 1915. Below, excursion boats heading to Rock Bluff Park were a common sight on the river, circa 1910.

team competitions— became popular following the construction of the boat house in west Ottumwa by the Ottumwa Oarsmen club just prior to 1900.

In 1909, the club hosted the Central States Amateur Rowing Association regatta. Another popular spot on the river was Rock Bluff Park located northwest of Ottumwa.

kelley's army

The river also brought what some people considered to be trouble. Ottumwa residents came face to face with Kelley's Army in 1894 when approximately 1,000 men, under the leadership of Charles T. Kelley and bound for the U.S. Capitol to protest unemployment and poor economic conditions, floated into the city limits on rafts.

Upon his arrival, Kelley sent the following letter to city officials:

"To the citizens of Ottumwa:
"Desiring to give my men a day in which to rest and clean

Members of Kelley's Army, below, making their way over the dam just west of Ottumwa, circa 1894.

up a bit, and desiring also not to appear improvident, I have requested Mr. Harry Lesson, of the Courier, to ask for 75 pounds of coffee and a quantity more of meat. Also to ask the tobacconists for such smoking and chewing tobacco as you can give.

"Yours, Chas. T. Kelley."

Hoping to discourage the protesters, whom most people of that day regarded as vagabonds and beggars, city fathers met with Kelley and agreed to provide his men with 1,500 loaves of bread, 1,500 pounds of bacon, 125 pounds of coffee, and 25 bushels of potatoes.

Originally, the men agreed to establish a camp near Garrison Rock, but they reneged and opted to stay near south Ottumwa. And, much to the dissatisfaction of some local citizens, the group held protest rallies in the park across from the courthouse. The group eventually joined forces with Coxey's Army, but the movement collapsed shortly after the men reached the White House.

Local historian H. L. Waterman, writing in 1914, describes Kelley's followers, below, as an "'army' of unemployed and n'er-do-wells."

During the 1903 flood a rowboat was manned near the Dain Manufacturing Company— the present site of the John Deere plant— in south Ottumwa.

Railroad workers rush to repair a segment of track that was washed away near Ottumwa in the 1903 flood.

An unknown photographer recorded this 1903 image from the safety of a horse-drawn wagon near Church and Sheridan streets in south Ottumwa.

the floods

Without a doubt, the most devastating characteristic of the meandering river was its ability to flood. Although the river surged over its banks almost annually, major floods were recorded in the years 1851, 1903, 1944, and 1947. If an 1878 history book is correct, Eddyville suffered the worst of the river's wrath in 1851 when the water level reached 37 feet. In 1903, as well as 1944, the river peaked at 19 feet.

The 1947 flood, often referred to as the granddaddy of all floods, proved the most devastating because of the economic losses suffered by the river towns of Eddyville, Chillicothe, Ottumwa and Eldon. That year, again at Eddyville, the highest water level was recorded at 27.8 feet.

The 1947 flood also spelled the beginning of the end for Central Addition, a residential area once boasting 650 lots and located in what is now the Greater Ottumwa Park. City officials strongly encouraged residents to move from the area, but many refused. Central Addition was not completely evacuated until 1955.

During the floods of the 1940s, U.S. Navy personnel stationed in Ottumwa were instrumental in evacuating residents and assisting in the efforts to build levees comprised of sand-

Residents of Central Addition, below, endured the river's recurring high waters and flooding, circa 1933.

bags.

After the 1947 catastrophe local officials began to earnestly investigate how to prevent another flood by rerouting the river. Earlier attempts to control the flooding were made, but they obviously proved ineffective. One project, in 1934, involved excavating the river bed to deepen the channel near the Market Street Bridge.

Members of the Ottumwa Red Cross operate a canteen service for local volunteer workers and military personnel during the 1944 flood.

U.S. Navy personnel, top left, launching boats for rescue work in Ottumwa during the 1944 flood. Top right, the Kresge five and dime store at the corner of Market and Main streets in Ottumwa during the 1947 flood. Below, one seasoned Ottumwa resident appears to take the 1947 flood in stride.

A determined group of Ottumwa men, linked by a safety rope, prepare to cross the Vine Street Bridge during the 1947 flood, according to the notation on the back of this photograph. Amid the devastation, an estimated 10,000 flood victims were evacuated from their homes and 30,000 residents were without electricity and safe drinking water.

Several attempts were made to establish an effective flood control system before the 1947 flood. Above, the river bed was excavated to deepen the channel just west of the Market Street Bridge in 1934.

Above, workers building the retaining wall by the municipal parking lot near the hydro dam in Ottumwa, circa 1930s.

Streetcars provided public transportation in Ottumwa for almost 50 years before they were replaced by city buses in 1930. Above, three electric streetcars converge near Franklin Park, or what is now Foster Park in east Ottumwa, circa 1905.

transportation

a viable transportation system proved to be the economic
lifeline of any city, town or community that would survive
and prosper in the Territory of Iowa and Wapello County.

Of course, railroads eventually emerged as the most effective means of transportation in the 1850s and remained at the
fore well into the next century. In addition, their presence precipitated Wapello County's industrial boom in the late 1800s by
fueling the coal mining industry and providing wholesale mar-
keters and manufacturers the means to transport products to distant cities.

However, early attempts to develop other transportation
systems preceded the steel rails.

The Des Moines River, deemed by speculators to be navigable by Mississippi River steamboats, despite the lack of a cor-
roborating survey, was considered the first logical area of development in the 1840s. But, for reasons examined in the previous
chapter, early attempts to establish a waterway failed.

plankroads and toll bridges

The construction of plankroads was another idea that fell to the wayside because of the looming railroads. As early as 1850, county residents met to raise money to build a plankroad from Ottumwa to Mt. Pleasant to intersect the Burlington and Mt. Pleasant Plankroad. Ottumwa entrepreneurs raised $8,700. Investors from Agency City and Ashland promised another $5,000 and $4,500, respectively, before the project was abandoned.

At Eddyville, a toll bridge was built across the Des Moines River in 1858. Constructed at a cost of $30,000, the bridge remained in operation until 1885 when it was destroyed by an ice gorge. It was replaced by a steel bridge in 1887 which was destroyed during the great flood of 1947. Wagon bridges were built in Chillicothe and Eldon in 1880 and 1892, respectively.

stagecoach lines

Stagecoaches also traversed the prairies prior to the arrival of the

The Ottumwa Buggy Company was a thriving business before the arrival of trains, streetcars and automobiles, circa 1890.

railroads. The Iowa Stage Company was based in Eddyville as early as 1848. Two years later, it was purchased by Frink, Walker & Co., which in turn sold the business to the Western Stage Company in 1853. By 1865, the stagecoaches traveled west to Plattesmouth, Nebraska some 200 miles away.

According to one map, stagecoaches traveled east from Eddyville with stops at Ottumwa, Agency, and Ashland before continuing on to Libertyville in Jefferson County. From Ottumwa, primary trails were established north through Dahlonega and Highland Center and then on to Hedrick, in Keokuk County, and south to Bloomfield in Davis County.

riding the steel rails

Railroad fever was burning in the early 1850s. The Des Moines River Valley Railroad was reportedly the first company to operate in Wapello County. Its agent was stationed at a depot located near Cliffland until 1855. The Burlington & Missouri River

A horse carriage provides a romantic means for courting. Pictured are Jim and Mattie Worrell near Ormanville, circa 1900. To fend off annoying insects, the horses are covered with fly netting.

Railroad Company (later, the Chicago, Burlington & Quincy Railroad) moved to Ottumwa in 1854 after county residents pledged more than $100,000 through the sale of bonds and another $40,000 in stocks. Five years later, the first train arrived in Ottumwa.

In effect, the laying of the steel rails through Wapello County guaranteed the future prosperity of Ottumwa and other towns. It is of little surprise that citizens courted railroad executives with economic incentives to entice prospective companies to their towns. In fact, some towns in the county were created by sheer virtue of the railroad's presence; others faced an inevitable death when bypassed.

In Competine Township, Farson was established in 1902 when the Chicago, Milwaukee & St. Paul Railroad tracks intentionally missed the existing town of Competine by a mere mile. Competine residents had little choice but to move their homes and other buildings to Farson.

Ashland, a major stop on the stagecoach line, once boasted a school, bank, brick yard, hotel, and a population of several hundred people before it bowed to nearby Eldon and the railroads in the 1870s. Once known as Ashland Crossing, Eldon became the railroad boom town of Washington Township in the late 1850s and 1860s when both the Chicago, Rock Island & Pacific Railroad and the Keokuk and Des Moines Railroad established branch offices in the town. Like their counterparts in Competine, Ashland residents followed the trains to Eldon.

Rock Island engine crew, opposite, preparing to leave Eldon, circa 1920.

The Rock Island Depot, opposite, in Ottumwa's east end, was open for business in 1911. Below, is the Chicago, Rock Island & Pacific Railroad's roundhouse in Eldon, circa 1905.

The two photographs above are examples of early train engine designs. Although the specific dates are not known, the images were more than likely recorded around Ottumwa just prior to the turn of the century. Right, the South Ottumwa Depot once located near the corner of Garfield and Sheridan Avenue. Among those pictured are William, Sarah Jane, Clara and Jack Wallace, circa 1900.

By 1888, five railroad companies operated within Wapello County accounting for 105 miles of track valued at $780, 803. The railroad industry continued to gain momentum into the next century and Ottumwa became home to a bustling rail yard. According to one account, 21 passenger trains passed through Ottumwa daily during the 1920s.

streetcars

At the local level, the horse-drawn streetcar first appeared on the avenues of Ottumwa in 1881. The first line, owned by Gen. John Morrow Hedrick, started at McPherson Street and extended east on Second Street to Market Street. By 1887, R. T. Shea's operation joined north and south Ottumwa.

Electric streetcars were in service by 1889. Although several companies were initially involved in the enterprise, by 1908 the Ottumwa Railway and Light Company established itself at the fore. It owned 17 streetcars and maintained 13 miles of track.

The advent and availability of gasoline and diesel-powered vehicles sounded the death knell for the oft-romanticized streetcars. They were replaced by city buses in 1930. In addition, the population became less dependent on the rails for passenger service as the nation began to develop its highway system.

early roads and highways

Eddyville reportedly had the first paved rural road in Iowa. Local farmers pooled their resources to pave, with cement, a sandy portion of the Currier Mill Road in 1908. Although the road is still in use today, it has been covered with asphalt. U. S. Highway 63 was paved in 1926. One year later, U. S. Highway 34 was paved through Agency, thus connecting Ottumwa and Fairfield.

During that period, according to one source, Ottumwa was the home of 14 different car dealerships which sold nearly every model available ranging from the Hudson to the Cadillac.

aviation

Wapello County never established itself as a major aviation market, but over the years several small commercial lines have located terminals at Ottumwa's airport. During World War II Ottumwa was selected as a location for a U.S. Naval Air Base.

Section workers, opposite page, employed by the Chicago, Burlington & Quincy Railroad, circa 1910.

Opposite, workers for the Chicago, Milwaukee & St. Paul Railroad, circa 1890.

The former Sherman Street Station on the Milwaukee Railroad line. The depot was located near what is now Gateway Drive in Ottumwa, circa 1915.

The Union Depot waiting room, complete with a spitoon and a concession counter, circa 1905

The west approach to Ottumwa's Burlington Depot— more commonly known as Union Depot, circa 1911. The brick structure was razed in 1949.

An electric streetcar descends Court Street near downtown Ottumwa, circa 1900. Below, workers use hand signs to direct heavy traffic during Ottumwa's 1923 Diamond Jubilee in honor of the city's 75th anniversary.

*Ottumwa Railway and
Light Company employ-
ees, circa 1908.*

Julian C. Manchester, a former proprietor of the Ballingall Hotel, tools down the streets of Ottumwa in his horseless carriage, circa 1900.

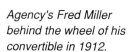

Agency's Fred Miller behind the wheel of his convertible in 1912.

A barnstormer's bi-
plane alit in a field
near Eddyville, circa
1915.

A modern-day aerial
photograph of the Ot
tumwa Municipal Air-
port just north of
Ottumwa. During World
War II, the U. S. Navy
used the facility as a
training air base.

In 1870, Ottumwan Allen Johnston invented the Johnston Ruffler, a sewing machine attachment. The success of that invention led to the establishment of the Johnston Ruffler Company and eventually the Ottumwa Iron Works. Right, an advertisement that appeared in the 1893 edition of the Ottumwa Courier's Annual Trade Edition.

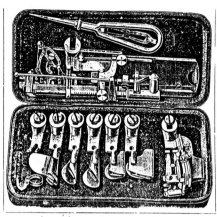

JOHNSTON'S
New Set of Attachments
FOR ANY SEWING MACHINE.

PERFECT IN WORKMANSHIP.

ELEGANT IN FINISH.

SATISFACTORY IN OPERATION.

THE **JOHNSTON RUFFLER** Co.

OTTUMWA IRON WORKS,

... ENGINEERS AND EXPERTS IN ...

Coal Hoisting, Hauling and Loading Machinery,

Geared and Direct Acting Hoisting Engines, Friction and Clutch Tail or Endless Rope Engines, Cars, Cages, Fixtures and Supplies.

Examinations made for Underground Haulage; Estimates Furnished Complete or in part; Machinery Erected and Started. Desired Output Guaranteed.

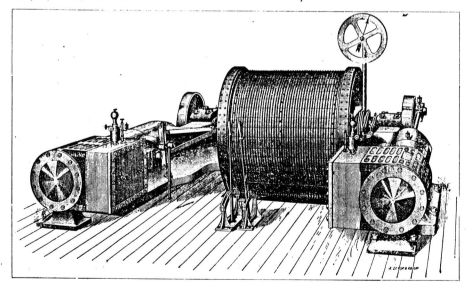

DIRECT ACTING DOUBLE HOISTING ENGINE.

industry
and business

Ottumwa— the transportation center, seat of government and the largest city in Wapello County— was the logical setting for the major industrial and business undertakings. The golden age of Ottumwa industry was in the late 1800s when every conceivable product from sewing paraphernalia to coal drilling implements to cigars were manufactured.

industry leaders

Some of the county's most enterprising industrialists were also great innovators. Ottumwan Allen Johnston was famous for his invention, the Johnston Ruffler, a sewing machine attachment. He and other local businessmen formed the Johnston Ruffler Company and the Ottumwa Iron Works in 1872. Roy Johnston and Frank W. Sharp founded the Johnston & Sharp Manufacturing Company in the early 1900s. It was sold in 1941 as the Johnston Lawn Mower Corporation.

Coal mining and farming also reflected major industrial in-

terests in early Wapello County. Although most coal mining operations had ceased by the 1920s, suffice it to say that southeast Iowa was the site of some of the state's richest coal veins. This provided the impetus for the construction of the famous Coal Palace in 1890 and other related industries.

Martin Hardsocg is credited with inventing a unique auger to bore coal as well as the celebrated black diamond pick. A German immigrant, he formed Hardsocg Manufacturing Company in 1879 and moved the operation from Avery to Ottumwa in 1885. The company, under the supervision of Lester Hardsocg, was sold to the Cardox Co. of Chicago in 1947. Changing hands again at a later date, it became the Long-Airdox Company.

joseph dain and john deere

Although the name John Deere is considered synonymous to the pioneering of farm machinery, it was Joseph Dain who owned and operated the first such company in Ottumwa.

Dain moved his plant to Ottumwa in 1900 from Carrollton,

Inventor Allen Johnston and, below, the home of the Johnston Ruffler Company and later the Ottumwa Iron Works, circa 1892.

Mo. His innovative engineering— especially in regard to hay loaders— had earned him a considerable reputation within the industry. In fact, Deere outlets even sold the Dain line. The two companies merged in 1910 to form what is now the John Deere Ottumwa Works.

cigar factories

The manufacture of cigars might seem like an unusual business interest to those unfamiliar with the early history of Ottumwa and Wapello County. However, in its heyday— at the turn of the century— the local industry included 16 different firms and employed more than 400 cigar makers.

New Yorker Daniel Morey established the first cigar factory shortly after his arrival in Ottumwa during 1871. The La Flor de Mayo proved to be the most popular cigar brand made by his company. Later he became the president of the Morey and Myers Cigar Company.

Most of the quality tobacco was imported from Havana, Cuba. Before the railroad freight lines were established, bales of

Martin Hardsocg, above, with his co-patented Nicholls carpenter square, circa 1905. Below, Hardsocg at age 70, circa 1922.

Workers at the Pallister Brothers cigar company are, left to right, Lloyd Tozer, Joe Vest, Harry Tozer, and one unidentified companion. Although this picture is not dated, the company conducted business in Ottumwa from 1888 to 1928.

Cigar manufacturer Julius Fecht, wearing hat, poses with employees, circa 1905. Fecht is often regarded as one of the major forces in the now-defunct cigar industry.

Julius Fecht moved his Ottumwa business to 302-306 W. Main St. in 1916. Fecht died in 1924, but the business survived until 1953.

Emma Turner, center, and her co-workers box cigars for the George Potter & Brother Cigar Factory in Ottumwa, circa 1924. Single women, hoping to find beaus, would sometimes include their names and addresses in the cigar boxes.

tobacco were shipped overland from Miami to Ottumwa with an armed escort. All of the cigars were then hand rolled, boxed and shipped throughout the Midwest.

Other tobacco concerns included the Wapello Cigar Company, Union Cigar Company, Bigham Cigar Factory and Pallister Brothers. The Ottumwa Cigar Box Company produced wooden containers for the various local enterprises. The Julius Fecht Cigar Company was the last cigar manufacturer in Ottumwa. After more than 70 years in business, it closed in 1953.

Other products made in Wapello County included linseed oil, candy, flour, beer and bricks.

the 1930s

Despite the Great Depression, a number of ancillary manufacturers emerged in the 1930s to accommodate the needs of thriving companies such as John Deere Ottumwa Works and John Morrell & Company.

The Ottumwa Foundry Inc., which opened in 1933, produced farm equipment for Deere while the Ottumwa Shipping Container Company manufactured corrugated containers for Morrell's. The Winger Manufacturing Company produced hand trucks, tables and conveyors for the packing house.

banking interests

Private banking interests in Ottumwa were first established in the late 1840s by the Temple brothers and, later, West B. Bonnifield. S. T. Caldwell offered a similar service in Eddyville beginning in the 1860s which was still in operation at the time of his death in 1878. Thomas Ping founded the Farmers and Merchants Bank of Ashland during the mid-1850s.

Bonnifield and a group of investors received a charter for the First National Bank of Ottumwa in 1863. Other early Wapello County banks were Iowa National Bank (1870), Ottumwa National Bank (1882), Ottumwa Savings Bank (1887), City Savings Bank (1888), Blakesburg Savings Bank (1890), Eldon Savings Bank (1895), Union Trust & Savings Bank (1898), Wapello County Savings Bank (1900), Manning & Epperson State Bank (1902), South Ottumwa Savings Bank (1903), Kirkville Savings Bank (1904), Citizens Savings Bank and Farson Savings Bank (1905), Agency Savings Bank (1906), and the Chillicothe Savings Bank (1907).

early newspapers

The *Des Moines Courier* was the first newspaper published in

The manufacturing of cigars was a laborious task as illustrated by this photograph inside an unidentified Ottumwa cigar factory, circa 1910.

Left, the former Iowa National Bank Building on the northeast corner of Market and Main streets in Ottumwa, circa 1900.

The Agency Savings Bank, immediately below, was established in 1906 at the corner of Main and Hazel streets in Agency.

The Blakesburg Savings Bank, established in 1890, folded during the Great Depression.

William B. Bonnifield holds a first-issue note from Ottumwa's First National Bank. Bonnifield's father, West B. Bonnifield, established the bank in 1863. It was the first national bank organized west of the Mississippi River.

Editors of yesteryear were actively involved in all facets of the operation. Above, Bert Davis of the Eldon Register sets the type by hand, circa 1916.

the county beginning Aug. 8, 1848. In 1857, the name was changed to the Ottumwa *Courier*. The Ottumwa *Daily Courier*, first published in 1865, was purchased by A. W. Lee in 1890. It was Lee who founded the Lee Newspaper Syndicate, an organization now known as Lee Enterprises Inc., of which the Ottumwa *Courier* is still a member.

The *Democratic Statesman* (1859) became the *Ottumwa Democratic Union* (1861) and, eventually, the *Democratic Mercury* (1861). Other newspapers were the *Copperhead* (1868), the *Ottumwa Democrat* and the *Reveille* (1870), the *Daily Democrat* (1874), the *Ottumwa Sun* and the *South Ottumwa News* (1890), the *Daily Republican* (1895), the *Independent* and the *Saturday Herald* (1899), and the *Labor News* (1912).

In Eddyville, the *Free Press*, first published in 1853, was renamed the *Commercial* in 1856. Other short-lived publishing ventures were the *Star* (1862), the *Independent* and the *Des Moines Valley Gazette* (1868), the *Advertiser* (1869) and the *Tribune* (1905).

The *Herald*, established in 1873, was the first Eldon newspaper followed by the *Messenger* (1875), the *Times*, which became the *Western News* (1876), the *Review* (1881), the *Graphic* (1891), the *Eldon Forum* (1893), and the *Register* (1912).

Editor Bert Davis and Mary Enyart prepare an edition of the Eldon Register, circa 1916. The newspaper was founded in 1912.

In 1896, Ottumwa grocers held their first annual picnic in Eldon.

Celania's store in downtown Ottumwa sold fresh fruit, ice cream, and homemade candy, circa 1897.

Mitchell & Seaburg Groceries, formerly located at 901 W. Second St. in Ottumwa, opened for business in 1908.

The J. H. Merrill Co. Wholesale Grocers delivery truck, circa 1915. The company began its operation in Ottumwa as early as 1872. The driver is not identified.

L. C. Neff owned and operated this grocery store at 620 Church St. in Ottumwa from 1895 to 1945.

The Edward Durbin and Son General Merchandise Store in Agency, circa 1905.

The Hagberg and Farrington Shoe Store at 134 E. Main St. in Ottumwa, circa 1906.

The well-groomed man of the early 1900s had a host of specialty shops designed to meet his needs. To the immediate right is the J. P. Anderson tailor shop in downtown Ottumwa, circa 1901. Pictured below is the Swastika Dress Club in Ottumwa, circa 1910.

Cobbler Roy Stevens, below, repairs a shoe while the customer waits, circa 1898.

Above, the interior of an Ottumwa tailor shop, circa 1900. Carl Swanson is seated at the lower left.

These gents while away the afternoon at the Ottumwa Brewing Co., date unknown.

Several small distilleries, such as the Ottumwa Brewing Co., catered to the local market, date unknown.

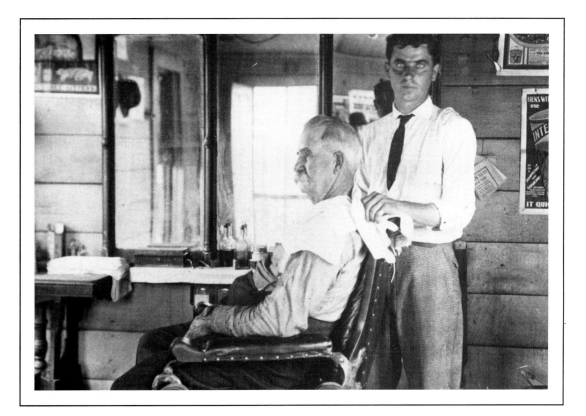

Barber Riley Staats, right, plying his trade in Ottumwa, circa 1917.

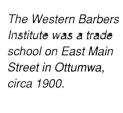

The Western Barbers Institute was a trade school on East Main Street in Ottumwa, circa 1900.

Bert McElroy owned and operated McElroy's Restaurant in downtown Ottumwa near the turn of the century.

Behind the scenes—the kitchen of McElroy's Restaurant.

James Smith purchased the South Side Bakery in 1910 after moving to Ottumwa from Carrollton, Mo. The business was located at 410 Church St. in south Ottumwa.

Earl Kirkhart was a driver for Lang's Bakery in Ottumwa, circa 1903. Of course, the largest baking firm in Ottumwa at this time was Lowenberg Bakery. Chris and Anton Lowenberg established the firm in 1875.

Herbert Young and Walt Burnett in 1905 at the Iowa Malleable Iron Works.

Realtor Ben Patsey and his son, Bernard, set up shop at 413 Church St., circa 1908.

Electric signs began to appear in downtown Ottumwa shortly after the turn of the century. The sign for Colonial Billiards, located at 213 E. Main, was installed in 1906. In addition, note the wooden water mains in the foregound.

Employees of the L. R. Steel Company Inc. at the firm's grand opening in Ottumwa, circa 1917.

Two early wholesale firms in Otumwa were the E. H. Emery Company, which sold fruit, and the Harper & McIntire Co., which specialized in hardware supplies, circa 1905.

Employees of R. N. Wilcox, General Black-smith, date unknown.

Employees of the Johnston & Sharp Manufacturing Company prior to 1900.

Hardsocg Manufacturing Company employees, circa 1909. Martin Hardsocg is sitting in the foregound holding a framing square.

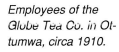

Employees of the Globe Tea Co. in Ottumwa, circa 1910.

The Hotel Ottumwa, built in 1917, still stands the corner of East Second and North Court streets operating as the Parkview Plaza.

The Frasier Hotel in downtown Ottumwa, circa 1915.

Peter Ballingall built the Ballingall House in 1864 at the corner of Main and Green streets in Ottumwa. The building is still standing.

The Hollenbeck Hotel, sometimes referred to as the Exchange Hotel, operated in Eldon during the late 1800s. The structure, built by William Hollenbeck, had 30 sleeping rooms.

The Rev. Allen Simpson was the first African American in Iowa to be ordained a Catholic priest. He presided over his first mass in 1948 at Sacred Heart Catholic Church in Ottumwa.

religion

"It may be a matter of interest to know who preached the first sermon in the county. I have sought in vain to ascertain this fact with certainty. The honor lies between J. H. D. Street, Joseph H. Flint, Silas Garrison, T. M. Kirkpatrick, Milton Jamison, B. A. Spaulding and Joel Harrington.

"I think, however, that the palm must be borne off by T. M. Kirkpatrick of the Methodist Episcopal Church, who, as I am informed by Seth Ogg, preached on the Keokuk prairie, on the south side of the river, just below Ottumwa, in an Indian wigwam, made of bark, early in 1843— just at what time Mr. Ogg could not inform me.

"I know that B. A. Spaulding, of the Congregational Church, preached in 1843 at Agency City and Ottumwa, but at what time I have not ascertained. He, however, preached in a log cabin, where Union Block now stands, and Kirkpatrick preached in a wigwam made of bark. I think the presumption is in favor of Rev. Mr. Kirkpatrick of the wigwam."

kirkpatrick and spaulding

All past historians agree with Judge Henry Bascomb Hendershott, who delivered the above speech to members of the Old Settlers' Association in 1874, that Kirkpatrick deserves the honor. However, Kirkpatrick and Spaulding were equally competent in establishing the early houses of worship in Wapello County.

Although Kirkpatrick began preaching in the area as early as 1843, a church was not formally organized in Ottumwa until 1845. He was instrumental in establishing the Methodist Episcopal churches in Eddyville, Kirkville, Agency City and Ashland.

Spaulding, a graduate of the Andover Theological Seminary in Massachusetts, was a member of the Iowa Band— a group of theologians who selected the Territory of Iowa as the place to begin their missionary work. Spaulding founded the Congregational Church of Ottumwa in 1846 where he preached for the next 22 years. It is interesting to note that the church adopted the following resolution in 1854: "Resolved, that neither slave-holders, *nor the apologists* of slave holding, shall be received in this church."

Both men experienced difficulty in forming the first congregations in the new territory. The population was sparse and many of the early pioneers were simply overwhelmed by the daily struggle to survive. Indeed, Spaulding's first congregation was comprised of a mere eight members. Shortly after arriving in the county, he sent the following letter to friends at the seminary:

"Prayer meetings have been held occasionally in various places. The population, however, is so scattered that it is much more difficult to sustain a prayer meeting here than in the East, though I cannot say with certainty that the moral or spiritual difficulty, judging from the very small number that I have sometimes seen assembled in populous villages, is any greater."

It is impossible to list all of the churches that have been organized over the years, but, generally, many of the early churches were established along ethnic lines by the various groups of immigrants who settled in Wapello County.

ethnic churches

The African Methodist Episcopal Church first met in 1867, although a building wasn't erected in Ottumwa until 1893. In 1875, the Swedish Evangelical Lutheran Church was also founded in Ottumwa, although it was reportedly first organized

In 1888 the Second African Baptist Church congregation purchased this building at the corner of Fourth and Green streets in Ottumwa. The building, which originally housed the First Presbyterian Church, was built in 1866. The picture on the opposite page was made about 1880.

in the village of Munterville as early as 1856. The Swedish Mission Church held its first service in 1869, but was not incorporated until 1886. That same year, the First German Evangelical Lutheran St. Paul's Church congregation began meeting in the Swedish Lutheran Church. The synagogue of B'Nai Jacob opened its doors for worship in 1915.

catholic churches

The first Roman Catholic Church was established at Ottumwa in the late 1840s. The initial church was known as St. Nicholas, according to one historian, but a specific date is not given. St. Mary's Catholic Church is the moniker normally associated with the church. The present church was completed in 1930.

In the town of Eddyville, St. Mary's Catholic Church was organized in 1848. St. Patrick's, in Ottumwa, dates back to 1879.

Sacred Heart was formed in 1897. Fifty-one years later,

The Swedish Evangelical Lutheran Church and Parsonage, circa 1885, once stood near the present location of the Swedish Lutheran Church in Ottumwa at the corner of Fourth and Jefferson streets. The church was organized in 1871, and its first pastor, the Rev. M. C. Ranseen, arrived in 1875.

SWEDISH EV. LUTHERAN CHURCH, OTTUMWA, I

Allen Simpson, of Ottumwa, the first African-American priest in Iowa, conducted his first mass in the church.

other early churches

Elsewhere around the county, the first Bladensburg Christian Church was erected in the early 1890s. A Seventh Day Adventist Church was also located in Bladensburg as early as 1898. Although not incorporated until 1894, records of the First Baptist Church of Blakesburg show that members met as early as 1846.

The Baptist Church of Competine, formed in 1867, was destroyed by fire in 1891. The new church was moved to Farson in 1908 and renamed the First Baptist Church of Farson. Worship began at Chillicothe's Methodist Church in 1860.

Mars Hill Baptist Church, still standing in southern Wapello County, was placed on the National Register of Historic Places in 1974. The log cabin church was reportedly built in 1856. The earliest grave in its cemetery is dated 1846.

Sacred Heart Catholic Church, right, was built in Ottumwa's east end in 1898. The rectory was completed the following year.

The above St. Mary's Catholic Church, built in 1860, was razed in 1929 to make way for the current structure at Fourth and Court streets in Ottumwa. Next to the church is the building that housed St. Joseph's Hospital from 1914 to 1924.

The First Methodist Episcopal Church at the corner of Fourth and Market streets in Ottumwa, circa 1909.

Members of the Bladensburg Christian Church in 1895 were, front row, left to right, J. D. Holmes (partially visible), Reuben Elmaker, Barney Muldoon, William Brown, T. B. Palmer, Elizabeth Spurlock, W. B. Spurlock, W. F. Parker, Maria Ryan, Samuel Ryan, Elijah Eggers, and Nancy Eggers. In the second row, left to right, are C. L. Walker (not visible), George R. Faucett, Eliza J. Faucett, Eliza Worley, Nancy Weaver, Lydia Lieuosy, Harriet A. Shepard, James Timonds, Eliza Timonds, Teresa Allen, J. M. J. Allen, Angeletta Smith, Catherine Murray, and W. D. Smith. The thrid row, left to right, includes, Nancy Williams, Sara J. Cole, John Cole, Mary E. McClung, S. B. McClung, Eliza J. Long, S. D. Long, Daniel Fulton, Norman Reno, Matilda Reno, L. D. Yeager, and Margaret Yeager. In the fourth row, left to right, are Thomas Traul, Ellona Bedwell, D. S. Bedwell, America McGuire, H. H. McGuire, Edmond M. Hanna, Joseph G. Hanna, J. S. Phillips, and John O'Bryant. The children are not identified.

The Rev. and Ellen Donohoo, circa 1900, were members of the United Brethren Church, according to the note on the photograph below. If the date and information are correct, the couple presided over a church that was moved to Ormanville in 1897. Later it was reorganized as a Methodist church. In the bottom photograph are members of the Highland Baptist Church Ladies Aid in Highland Township, circa 1917.

The Rev. and Mrs. Stilson, below, celebrate their 50th wedding anniversary, circa 1917. They were associated with St. Mary's Episcopal Church.

Pictured above are choir boys from the Trinity Episcopal Church in Ottumwa, circa 1896. Art Lowenberg is standing in the first row on the far right. The choirmaster, Thomas H. Gorman, is holding young Florence Dimmitt.

The Loyal Boys, above, were students from the First Christian Church Sunday School in Ottumwa, circa 1900.

The Baptist Church of Competine, left, and its parsonage, below, were moved to Farson in 1908. The move was precipitated by the decision of a Chicago, Milwaukee and St. Paul Railroad surveyor to bypass Competine and establish the nearby town of Farson in 1902. Family members posed in front of the parsonage are not identified.

*The Kirkville Methodist
Church, circa 1909.*

*The First Baptist
Church of Ottumwa,
circa 1909.*

Members of Ottumwa's Baptist Church Choir, circa 1892.

Mars Hill Baptist Church, still standing in southern Wapello County, was placed on the National Register of Historic Places in 1974.

*The second Adams
School in Ottumwa,
left, was built in 1883
after the original school
was deemed unsafe,
circa 1883.*

education

"The safety and perpetuity of our Republican institutions depend upon the diffusion of intelligence among the masses of people. The statistics of the penitentiaries and alm-houses (poorhouses) throughout the country show that education is the best preventative of crime. They also show that the prevention of these evils is much less expensive than the punishment of one and the relief of the other."

Iowa Gov. James Grimes presented that social mandate in his 1854 inaugural speech, but the first private school in Wapello County had already opened its doors to students eight years earlier. Classes were held in the county courthouse located at Third and Market streets.

Private schools were also operating in Dahlonega, Agency and Eddyville in the 1840s.

ashland seminary

The Ashland Seminary was established in the town of Ashland, near what is now Cardinal High School, by the Methodist Episcopal Church in 1854. Rev. Lewis Dwight was named principal. Although early accounts state that 84 male and 52 female students paid tuition during the 1857-58 school year, the institution struggled to survive. An embezzlement scandal that same year reportedly forced the school to close indefinitely. Bricks from the seminary were used to build the Ashland School in 1886.

public schools in ottumwa

The advent of the public school system in Ottumwa can be traced to the first recorded meeting of the Directors of Ottumwa City School District on May 15, 1858. Three days later the board secured, free of rent, classroom space in the Methodist Episcopal Church. Classes were to be held there until monies could be raised to finance the building of a schoolhouse.

Evidently, the early public schools were not too popular among prospective students. Dr. W. L. Orr complained to the

The third high school in Ottumwa, below, was built in 1899 at West Fourth and Ottumwa streets. The building, which eventually housed Washington Junior High, cost $50,000 to build.

board of directors "that a number of scholars were so irregular in their attendance as to very materially interfere with the progress of classes." To solve the problem, the directors voted to publish in the city's newspapers an appeal to parents to send their children to school. Later that year, after lengthy debate, the directors adopted the nine-month school year over other proposals that included six and 10-month terms.

It wasn't until 1865 that construction was completed on the first Adams School, located on College Square— the site of the present high school. By 1878, Lincoln and Douglas schools were in operation and the high school students met on the top floor of the Adams School. The district employed 27 teachers that year. The second Adams School was built in 1883 on the same site as the original building.

Ottumwa schools were segregated until 1871. African-American students attended classes in a building on Center Avenue beginning in 1865. Two years later, classes were held in

Classes were first held in the current Ottumwa High School in 1923. It is located on the same site as the original Adams School built in 1865.

Ottumwa High School's 1920 graduates at their class picnic.

Members of the Ottumwa High School class of 1905 at their reunion in either 1940 or 1945.

the African Methodist Episcopal Church until integration was approved.

A new high school was built in Ottumwa in 1899 at West Fourth and Ottumwa streets. The original building, which eventually became Washington Junior High, cost $50,000. The vacant building was destroyed by fire in 1990. The current high school was built adjacent to the old Adams School in 1923. In fact, the original Adams School bell, dating back to 1869, is now located on the grounds of today's high school. It was salvaged from the second Adams School when it was razed in 1929. Froebel School, once located directly behind the Adams School, was torn down in 1919 to make way for the new high school.

blakesburg and agency

Blakesburg's first school opened in 1851, but it wasn't until 1922 that a class graduated from the town's first four-year high

The Agency Public School, below, was built in 1893. It was the town's first school to have steam heat.

school.

In Agency, a new school was built in 1938 by the Public Works Administration, a federal jobs program created to ease unemployment during the Great Depression.

rural schools

By 1930 there were 96 rural schools in Wapello County. Examples of early rural schools included Brush Creek School, first organized in a log cabin prior to 1870 in Adams Township, and Cross Roads School, once located just north of Agency, which opened in 1869. Upon graduating from eighth grade, rural students who wished to continue their education had to attend the nearest town's high school.

Four country schools were moved to Farson in 1922 in an early attempt at consolidation. Due to a lack of financing, the consolidation was dissolved in 1924. Three rural schools— Competine, Concord and Cedar— were returned to their original sites the following year. The fourth, Lowell School, was sold and torn down. Most rural school buildings were abandoned following the consolidation of Iowa's independent school districts

Agency elementary students, circa 1921.

in the 1950s.

catholic schools

The Visitation Academy was the first Catholic school in Ottumwa. Strictly a girls' school, it was opened in 1858. As early as 1869 there was a Catholic school in Eddyville. Sacred Heart was established in Ottumwa in 1882 while St. Patrick's, in south Ottumwa, first held classes in 1929. The first Ottumwa Heights College, now the site of Indian Hills Community College, was completed in 1913. Fire destroyed the building in 1957. The class of 1930 was the first to graduate from Catholic Central High School.

business colleges

Wapello County also boasted several business colleges. The Ottumwa Business College held classes from 1871 to 1926 followed by the Iowa Success School which was started in 1908 and remained in operation until 1967.

A detailed account of the county's school system can be found in Ruth Sterling's 1986 book, *Wapello County History*.

Cross Roads School, formerly located one and one-half miles north of Agency, was built in 1906.

Brush Creek School, formerly located in Adams Township, was built in 1875. Pictured above are students and school officials on the last day of classes in 1888.

Center School was located near Bidwell, a former coal mining town five miles west of Ottumwa in Polk Township. The above picture was made in 1906.

Pictured below, left to right, are Daisy Baker Nash, Emma McCullough, Lucy Warden Brockman and Annie Peters Burkland. The ladies taught at Hedrick School in Ottumwa, circa 1891.

Competine teacher John F. Hankammer, left, circa 1903.

In the above photograph are the eighth grade graduates of the Wapello County rural school system, circa 1925.

Teachers, students and area residents rush to remove valuables from Rutledge School in Center Township. The fire destroyed the building, circa 1941.

Construction of the original Ottumwa Heights College, circa 1911. The Catholic school, completed in 1913, was destroyed by fire in 1957. Formerly located in north Ottumwa, the site is now occupied by Indian Hills Community College.

Eldon's Lincoln School was built in 1888. The four-room building housed all of the town's students. To the left are Mrs. Ayres' and Kate Kehm's students, circa 1889.

1891 high school graduates of Adams School in Ottumwa.

Students of Froebel School in Ottumwa, circa 1884. The school, built to accommodate the student overload at Adams School, was razed in 1919.

Adams School students, right, in 1913. In the back row on the far left is Evelyn Eaton. In the same row, second from the right, is Herman Swanson. The man with the beard is Mr. Boston, the custodian.

Hedrick School, built in 1890, was located in Ottumwa's west end on Summit Street. The students at the right attended the school in 1913.

The Chillicothe Public School, circa 1912.

Pictured, but not identified in order, are Sammy Blake, Loren Chisman, Harold Hamilton, Anna Howard, John Lundborg, Harold Phillips, Bert Sauer, Frank Sherman, Claire Sumner, Inez Collings, Katherine Travis, Mamie Darner, Vera Dougherty, Lela Hall, Irene Hugus, Hazel Lehman, Ollie Mathies, Virgil Bryant, Gracie Musgrove, Francis Oswalt, Marry Ruffing, Katie Schwartz, Gladys Shahan, Helen Stancer, Leila Stewart, Verl Harlan, and Alice Grider. The students attended Irving School in Ottumwa, circa 1891.

The original Aggasiz School, right, was built in 1892 on Ottumwa's south side. Initially, it was named Bryant School.

The writing on the back of the photograph above identifies the group as the Washington High School Orchestra. Considering the apparent age of the students, more than likely the writer actually meant the Washington Junior High Orchestra. The former high school on West Fourth and Ottumwa streets became the junior high school in 1923.

In this Norman Rockwell-like portrait are, left to right, Opal, Frank and Grace Arnold.

people

While some are either famous or infamous, others are destined to remain nameless in the annals of time. But, whether eking out a living from the land, toiling in a factory, raising a family, or heading a local industry, each and every resident has lent a firm hand in molding Wapello County's history.

Accordingly, this chapter contains many photographs of local citizens that were secured from the archives of the Wapello County Historical Society. Although it was impossible to accurately identify or date each photograph, almost all of the images bear the studio logos of past local professional photographers. This suggests that, more than likely, the subjects lived in Wapello County at one time or another. The images are included because they reflect the fashions, attitudes and moods of bygone days.

familiar names
Some past residents' familial ties are worthy of note. John B.

Archie Alphonso Alexander, opposite page, top left, was born on the south side of Ottumwa in 1888. He became the governor of the Virgin Islands in 1954.

Hugh and Martha Brown, opposite page, center, were among the early residents of Ottumwa. Hugh served as the Wapello County Clerk of Court in 1860.

The group portrait on the opposite page includes several of Ottumwa's leading businessmen and civic leaders near the turn of the century. Pictured are, front row, left to right, Belle Fiedler, Jennie Calhoun, Elizabeth Simmons, Jean Von Schrader, and Stella Sax. The back row includes, left to right, John Calhoun, J. B. Sax, Kitty Springer, Frank Von Schrader, Frank Simmons, and William Fiedler. Sax and Von Schrader were among the county's early bankers.

Pike, the proprietor of a Kirkville sawmill in the 1870s and, reportedly, the nephew of explorer Zebulon Montgomery Pike— for whom Colorado's Pike's Peak is named— is buried in Kirkville's West View Cemetery. Rumor has it that the explorer's brother is also buried there, but his gravestone could not be found. Local residents could not verify the story.

Sarah Harrison, who married Ottumwan James D. Devin, was the sister of Benjamin Harrison. Her brother, the 23rd president, visited Ottumwa in 1890.

New York artist John Mulvaney, visiting his brother, Peter, in Eldon during 1870, reportedly made preliminary sketches of an actual trial that took place during his stay. Six years later, his painting, *A Horse Thief Trial*, sold for $20,000 at the Centennial Exposition in Philadelphia.

However, the current owner of the painting, Joseph Szymanski of Beverly Hills, Calif., disputes its ties to Eldon, according to an article by Eldon historian Helen Glasson. Even though local historians have identified some of the residents portrayed in the painting, Szymanski claims that the work is based on a similar incident in Kansas.

Skimming through a county history book, one will even come across the name of journalist Horace Greeley, who, in 1887, became the first editor of the Eddyville *Tribune*. Despite the irony of sharing the same name and profession, he is not to be confused with the same Horace Greeley who coined the phrase, "Go west young man."

politics, literature and more art

Those who passed through Wapello County on their way to fame included engineer and politician Archie Alphonso Alexander, writer Edna Ferber, and artist Grant Wood.

Born on Ottumwa's south side in 1888, Alexander lived there for 11 years before his family moved to Des Moines. The first African-American engineering student— and football player— at the State University of Iowa, Alexander enjoyed a successful engineering career before entering politics. He became the governor of the Virgin Islands in 1954.

Ferber, winner of the Pulitzer Prize, lived in Ottumwa for seven years beginning in 1890. *Giant*, *So Big*, and *Show Boat* are among her credits.

Wood, of course, gained fame for painting the *American Gothic* while living in Eldon during 1930. Grant posed his sister, Nan Wood Graham, and his dentist, Cedar Rapids resident B. H. McKeeby, in front of the famous Gothic House. The modest

In the top photograph on the opposite page are, left to right, Eldon lawyers Earl Henry, W. D. Davis, Mr. Henshaw, Paul Ramseyer and Adelbert Christy, circa 1915.

In the photograph on the immediate left, opposite page, are members of the 1896 Eldon City Council. The men are Ed Harward, foreground; Tim Madden, George Earhart and William Knouff in the center row, left to right; and W. H. Stauffer and J. O. Hunnel in the back row, left to right.

Pictured on the bottom of the opposite page is a picnic organized for local lawyers and their respective families, circa 1900.

house has been on the National Register of Historic Places since 1974 and serves as the centerpiece for Eldon's Gothic Days celebration. The original painting can be seen at the Chicago Art Institute.

inventors

Several innovators resided in Ottumwa. Allen Johnston received more than 150 patents for his inventions. The Johnston Ruffler, a sewing machine attachment, is his most famous creation. Mrs. Honore Potts was also awarded a patent for her sad irons which were equipped with removable handles to prevent burns.

Martin Hardsocg formed Hardsocg Manufacturing Company to produce state-of-the-art coal augers and black diamond picks prior to 1900. The Hardsocgs also co-owned Nicholls Manufacturing Company, maker of the Nicholls Framing Square.

military service

Although Jonathan Woody, whose gravestone is in the Dahlonega Cemetery, is reportedly the only Revolutionary War veteran buried in the county, many residents served in the Grand Army of the Republic during the Civil War.

A fascinating 1905 letter by former Ottumwan Charles P. Brown recounts a Civil War battle at Blue Mills Ferry, near Liberty, Mo., in 1861. According to Brown, after an hour of fierce fighting the outnumbered Union forces suffered heavy losses—120 were killed or wounded. Brown was among the injured.

A corporal at the time of the battle, Brown later wrote, "Death was as near as a neighbor on that afternoon as any time in the war, and until the final 'hour and article' will never be any nearer."

Ottumwa physician Seneca B. Thrall served under Gen. Ulysses S. Grant during the siege of Vicksburg. Thrall's chess board— the only one in camp— provided entertainment for the future president, according to a 1935 Ottumwa *Courier* story.

Schaefer Field, in Ottumwa, is named after Walter B. Schaefer who was wounded in 1918 and later died in a German hospital. The Ottumwa chapter of the Veterans of Foreign Wars also bears his name. Blakesburg claims Vice Adm. William Schoech. He served in World War II and the Korean conflict before assuming command of the 7th Fleet while in Hawaii.

those who live in infamy

The infamous also made their presence known. Benjamin

World War I inductees in front of the Ottumwa Public Library in 1918.

World War I inductees in front of the Ottumwa Public Library in 1918.

Decoration Day memorial, circa 1927. The day of remembrance is now known as Memorial Day.

Local families and friends watch as their loved ones prepare to leave Ottumwa during World War I.

A fallen Wapello County soldier is laid to rest during World War I.

World War I veterans parading down the streets of Ottumwa, circa 1918.

McComb, found guilty for the murder of Laura Harvey, was the first person to be legally executed in the county. Although he escaped the wrath of two lynch mobs and avowed his innocence on the gallows, he was hanged Feb, 17, 1865. John Scott Smith, after confessing to the murder of Ottumwa policeman Albert M. Logan in 1875, did meet his fate at the hands of a lynch mob.

In 1910, John Junkin was hanged at Ft. Madison State Penitentiary after being convicted for a murder that took place at the corner of Camille and Gara streets in Ottumwa. Wapello County Sheriff Billie Jackson witnessed the execution.

Other cheerless moments in local history evolve around the Ku Klux Klan. On more than one occasion, the racist group marched through downtown Ottumwa during the 1920s.

clubs and organizations

Secret societies, fraternal organizations, and civic groups have always been popular in Wapello County. In 1847, plans were

John Junkin, below, was convicted of murder in Ottumwa and hanged at Ft. Madison State Penitentiary, circa 1910. Wapello County Sheriff Billie Jackson reportedly witnessed the execution, but he is not identified in the photograph.

made to form Ottumwa Lodge, No. 9, of the Independent Order of Oddfellows. The lodge became a reality the following year. Eddyville's I.O.O.F. Lodge obtained a charter in 1850. The first Masonic organization, Ottumwa Lodge, No. 16, dates back to 1848. An organizational meeting for the Young Men's Christian Association was first held in 1887.

A sampling of other groups organized over the years include the Wapello Club, Knights of Pythias, Grand Army of the Republic, Elks Club, American Legion, Veterans of Foreign Wars and Rotary Club.

Among the early sororities were the Shakespeare Club, founded in 1882, and the Woman's Suffrage Society, organized in 1886. Chartered in 1887, the Ottumwa Cloutman Corps #134, of the Woman's Relief Corps, remains active today as does Ottumwa's Young Women's Christian Association which was established in 1894. The Oakdale Woman's Club first met in 1915 followed by the Republican Women's Party in 1923.

Members of the Ku Klux Klan in a funeral procession in downtown Ottumwa, circa 1924.

Members of the Ottumwa Rotary Club in front of the John Morrell & Company office building, circa 1933.

Members of the Ottumwa Elks Club at the corner of Green and Second streets, circa 1920s.

The Woodmen of the World Degree Team, circa 1933.

In 1898, the Ottumwa YMCA Directors were, front row, left to right, A. D. Moss, J. T. Hackworth, T. D. Foster, Maj. Samuel Mahon and William McNett. The second row includes, left to right, J. Peach, Charles Hallberg, Dr. Edgeny, C. J. Ekfelt and Christopher Haw.

Dr. Paul Caster practiced an unorthodox brand of hands-on medicine— he was a healer. He arrived in Ottumwa in 1868 and built the Caster House Medical Infirmary, above, in 1874. The building, located at East Main and Cherry streets, was sold in 1894 and re-opened as the Ottumwa Hospital later that year.

Dr. Clyde A. Henry, a rural physician who began his practice near Competine in 1897, is pictured with his wife, Grace, circa 1912. Like many local physicians of his day, Henry graduated from the Keokuk Medical College. Below, Henry, third from left, and his classmates examine a cadaver, circa 1897.

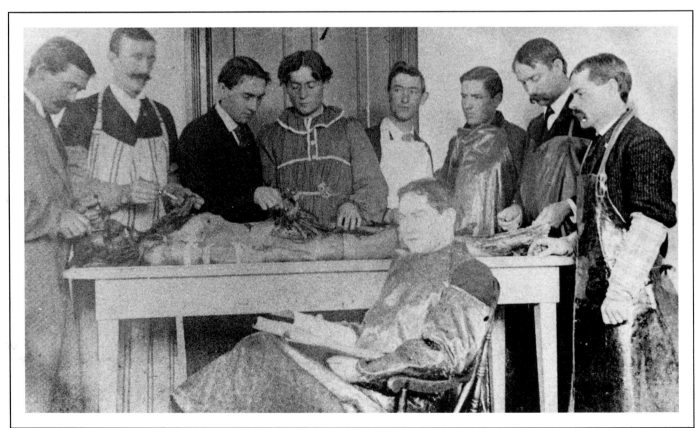

Graduates of the St. Joseph School of Nursing in Ottumwa, date uncertain. The school opened in 1914 and closed in 1971.

Dr. Gage C. Moore, standing, was the first African-American physician in Ottumwa. He is pictured with his wife, Emily, and their daughters, Jo Anne, seated, and Marie. Mrs. Moore's father, Fielding Johnson, is seated in the middle. This picture was made in 1942.

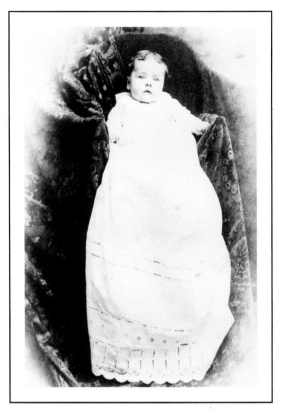

A long, flowing gown proved to be a stylish accessory for a portrait of the baby at the far left, circa 1900. In the photograph to the immediate left, young Francis Throsor appears somewhat frustrated by the size of her doll.

Lorne Hern at the piano in the family parlor.

The young girls at the right strike a tentative pose.

Bicycling was popular prior to the turn of the century as indicated by the two young men, top right, who use an unusual studio prop to recreate a racing atmosphere. Johnny Biltzgen, bottom right, brought along his banjo. Ottumwa resident William Harper, below, is pictured with his teddy bear, circa 1907.

The ladies above posed for Ottumwa photographer Loren Chisman who purchased the Guy Reid Studio in 1921.

Furs and parasols were popular among fashionable young ladies of the past. The date on the photograph directly above is 1901.

Mrs. Harlan Bruneutel, right, lets down her hair. Above, "Smithy" marks her 17th wedding anniversary with this portrait dated Feb. 6, 1913.

A wedding party, left, before the turn of the century.

Pictured below, left to right, are John, Watson, Mary and James Enyart in front of their Agency home, circa 1855.

Pictured above is the L. Caldwell family.

Thomas Reifsnyder and Fredericka Ehrmann on their wedding day, circa 1895.

The George J. Bennett family, below, of Richland Township. Their farm was located near Kirkville.

Mr. and Mrs. Jacob McCoy, above, on his 90th birthday.

The Andrew Swanson family lived at this house, left, on Grant Street in Ottumwa. Pictured left to right are Miss Nelson, Emily Elliott, Mrs. Andrew Swanson and Caroline Swanson.

An early home owned by the Ayres family of Agency.

Several presidents have visited Wapello County over the years. Among them were Ulysses S. Grant, Benjamin Harrison, William McKinley, William Howard Taft, Warren Harding, Harry Truman and Jimmy Carter. Richard Nixon lived in Ottumwa during the 1940s while he was stationed at the U.S. Naval Air Base north of the town. Above, Theodore Roosevelt at the Eldon Big 4 Fair in 1904.

Outfielder R. F. Bailey played baseball for the 1890 Coal Palace Team in Ottumwa.

leisure
activities

Whether playing baseball, watching the races, attending a performance at the opera house, or taking a sleigh ride to Garrison Rock, Wapello County residents have enjoyed a host of sports and leisure activities over the years.

baseball

Baseball was as popular before the turn of the century as it is to-day. Almost every town sponsored at least one team. Ottumwa's two earliest teams, the Actives and the Appanoose, were organized around 1867. The latter reportedly whipped the Highland De Sotas 136-29 in a game played July 1, 1871. Both teams played without gloves, but the losers also played barefooted.

The Coal Palace Team played in 1890. Other teams of that era were the Laddsdale Owls, the Reveal Stars and the North Stars. During the 1920s, fans could watch Mississippi Valley League action, or the Ottumwa Browns, an African-American team, at the Mississippi Valley Ball Park on West Second Street.

Members of the Reveal Stars were, front row, left to right, Howard Kesselring, Hugh Brown, Clyde Wilson, Manager Frank Kesselring and Boone Redburn. In the back row, left to right, are Paul Brown, Albert Wilson, Unknown, Horace Wilson and Fred Wilson. The players lived near Reveal School on Highway 23 northwest of Ottumwa, circa 1908.

The Ottumwa North Stars baseball team, circa 1900.

off to the races

Horse racing attracted large audiences to the opening of the Ottumwa Mile Track Association in 1895. More than four hundred entries participated in the event which attracted spectators from across the country. Horse races were also popular at the Wapello County Fair.

Kite Track in south Ottumwa provided bicycling enthusiasts the opportunity to witness world class competitors. Ottumwa's own Orlando Stevens was a world champion and held records in the unpaced mile, half-mile and quarter mile races near the turn of the century. The sport was also a popular high school track and field event. For those who demanded even more speed, Ottumwa also had a motorcycle club as early as 1913.

Bike races at the Kite Track on Ottumwa's south side, circa 1890.

theaters of yesteryear

Opera house owners hosted community cultural events ranging

Bicycling found its way into high school sports around the turn of the century. To the right is the 1902 Ottumwa High School track team.

The 1913 Ottumwa "Motor Cycle Club"— ready for a run.

Above, modern cycling outfits, circa 1900.

from high school graduations and theater performances to boxing and political rallies. The McHaffey Opera House in Eldon, built in 1891 with a seating capacity of 600, was still used for Eldon High School commencements until 1941. The Fritz Opera House was located above Fritz Hardware in Blakesburg while Thomas and John Lloyd managed Lloyd's Opera House in Kirkville. The Grand Opera House served Ottumwa.

The Chautauqua Circuit, organized just after the Civil War, brought many famous lecturers, entertainers and musicians to Wapello County up until the 1920s. Local entertainers also performed throughout the area. During the 1920s, actors Neal and Carolyn Shaffer, of Ottumwa, formed their own traveling comedy troupe around two popular characters, Toby and Susie. Movie theaters hastened the demise of the opera houses and traveling shows as residents flocked to local theaters to see motion pictures.

coal palace

The completion of the renowned Coal Palace in 1890, built to promote local industry, focused the national spotlight on Ottumwa when President Benjamin Harrison visited the remarkable structure. The brainstorm of Peter Ballingall, the building stood just northwest of the Union Depot and measured 200 feet high, 230 feet long and 130 feet wide. Its facade was made from blocks of coal.

Inside, visitors could view a splendid waterfall that emptied into a small lake, or enjoy a show in the auditorium that housed anywhere from 4,000 to 6,000 people. Beneath the structure, a Disneyland-like replica of a working coal mine, complete with mule cars and carbide lights, also proved to be a popular exhibit. The building was razed after the 1891 extravaganza.

The Agency Homecoming and the 1901 Old Settlers' Reunion were held at Fullen Grove, a favorite gathering spot along what is now the Hedrick-Agency Highway. The Agency Fair reportedly had the largest fairgrounds in the state before it was discontinued in the 1880s or 1890s. In Blakesburg, the Corn Carnival, which began in 1905, attracted more than 3,000 people in 1938. Ottumwa's 1923 Diamond Jubilee marked that town's 75th anniversary.

music

Municipal bands provided yet another source of entertainment. Perhaps the most famous was the Iowa National Guard 54th Regiment Band. Prior to 1903, the band played as the Wapello

The Grand Opera House— often referred to as the Ottumwa Opera House— was completed in 1891.

The McHaffey Opera House in Eldon, circa 1891.

Chief Band which had evolved from Schwabkey's Band. Professor C. F. T. Schwabkey organized the original band in 1865. The Kirkville Brass Band formed in 1884 followed by Wilson's Silver Band, in Eldon, during 1892.

On an individual note, Agency's Harold Ayres, a violin virtuoso at age 5, performed his first concert at the Grand Opera House in 1906. As an adult, he served as concertmaster for the Minneapolis Symphony for 15 years.

garrison rock

Garrison Rock and Horse Thief Cave, south of Agency near Cliffland, have always been popular destinations for day hikers. During the winter, it was also common to see horse-drawn sleighs making the trip at the turn of the century.

Many local history buffs still make the sojourn to Garrison Rock because of its ties to Ft. Sanford, the former outpost of the dragoons. It is also the site of one of the county's oldest cemeteries. Legend has it that horse thieves used the nearby cave to hide from authorities.

A boxing match in 1928 draws a crowd at the Grand Opera House in Ottumwa.

*Agency's Harold Ayres
performed at the Grand
Opera House in Ot-
tumwa in 1906 at
age 5.*

Traveling theater groups and entertainers of every variety often traveled from town to town to perform. Above is a show truck owned by Ottumwa's Leslie Patsey, circa 1902.

The South Ottumwa Band was one of many community bands organized throughout Wapello County.

The Iowa National Guard 54th Regiment Band from Ottumwa, circa 1903.

Parades have always been a popular source of local entertainment. Left, the Ottumwa Concrete & Tile Company's entry in the 1908 Labor Day Parade.

As the automobile inevitably replaced the horse and buggy, touring the countryside on a lazy summer became a favorite pastime, circa 1915. Sue Swirls is sitting in the center.

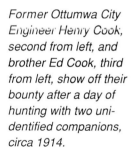

Former Ottumwa City Engineer Henry Cook, second from left, and brother Ed Cook, third from left, show off their bounty after a day of hunting with two unidentified companions, circa 1914.

The Ottumwa Coal Palace, the brainchild of Col. Peter Ballingall, was built in 1890 to promote local industry. The structure, which included a replica of an underground coal mine, was visited by Presidents Benjamin Harrison and William McKinley. Located near the Union Depot, the Coal Palace was dismantled shortly after the 1891 exhibition.

Although it appears as if they are wearing padded football pants, the young men above won the 1901-02 YMCA basketball championship in Ottumwa.

Ladies from Ottumwa's First Methodist Church were responsible for organiz-
ing the YWCA in 1894. In addition to sponsoring activities, the association op-
erated a boarding house for young women. Pictured above are members of a
1907 basketball team.

Dick Perdew, left, was the captain of the 1920 Ottumwa High School football team. Immediately below, members of the 1915 OHS football team. Coached by Wilber Vaughn, the first team included Carl Hampton, quarterback; Eugene Swanson, center; Maurice Speivak and Edwen Sequist, guards; Leo Rater and William Woodrow, tackles; and Arthur Griffin at the halfback position. At the bottom of the page is the 1907 OHS team.

The above photographs show the construction of the Ottumwa Municipal Pool— the largest in Iowa when it opened in 1929.

The annual pet show at the Ottumwa Public Library. The Ottumwa Library Association was incorporated in 1872 and Samuel Mahon served as its first president. Philanthropist Andrew Carnegie contributed $50,000 toward the construction of the existing building in 1900. Locally, Col. Peter Ballingall provided another $6,000 while J. T. Hackworth made the library the principal beneficiary of his estate. The Eldon Public Library received $7,500 from the Carnegie trust.

By today's standards, tennis wear has changed dramatically since this photograph was made of an early tennis club.

The gentlemen at the left ham it up for the camera while enjoying a "picnic," circa 1900.

Rock Bluff Park, along the Des Moines River between Ottumwa and Eddyville has long been a favorite spot for county residents to enjoy an afternoon.

The Wapello Club, above, dates back to 1893. The social organization limited its membership roll to 150.

The Ottumwa Country Club, below, opened in 1906. The building was destroyed by fire in 1947 and rebuilt the following year.

A few hearty residents braved the winter cold to visit Horse Thief Cave east of Ottumwa, circa 1896.

Enjoying a sleigh ride near Garrison Rock, circa 1896. These classic winter photographs were made by C. B. Hughes, a member of the Ottumwa YMCA Camera Club.

credits

The following people and organizations contributed photo-graphs for publication in this book:

chris d. baker
irene baker
the late pauline davis
lucille doughty
deb dyer
jo eddy
katie foglesong
leroy follett
mariam goughnour
beverly graham
wanda graham
raymond griggs
leslie heemsborgen
shirley inman
iowa historical society

barbara kent
paul kesselring
mike lemberger
ben mirgon
blanche morgan
catherine newquist
ottumwa public library
ottumwa water works
cora paxton
dale paxton
edith reed
nancy vaughn renville
charles robinson
lucille roth
marilyn sedore
mary sharp
the late allen sharp
betty smith
charles smith
david staats
ruth sterling
jo moore stewart
thelma swanson
bruce turner
helen vaughan
carol vivian
m. andrew walden
howard wallace
wapello county genealogical society
wapello county historical society

bibliography

books

Annual Trade Review of the Ottumwa Courier. Chicago: Manz & Co., 1893.

Evans, S. B., *History of Wapello County, Iowa and Representative Citizens*. Chicago: Biographical Publishing Company, 1901

Harding, Alvie and Mable, *The Ghost Mining Town of Laddsdale, Iowa, 1872-1918*. Ottumwa: Ottumwa Printing, 1971.

History of Wapello County, Iowa. Chicago: Western Historical Company, 1878.

Our Town Eddyville, 1840-1990. Baltimore: Eddyville Historical Society, 1990.

Sterling, Ruth, *History of Wapello County*. Montezuma: Sutherland Printing Company, Inc., 1986.

Taylor, James C., *Ottumwa: One Hundred Years A City*. Chicago: Manz Corp., 1948.

Waterman, Harrison L., *History of Wapello County, Iowa.*
        Chicago: S. J. Clarke Publishing Company, 1914.

manuscript collections

Agency, Iowa Scrapbook. Ottumwa Public Library.
Brown, Charles P. Letter, 1912. Ottumwa Public Library.
McClung, Samuel Brown, Diary, 1852-55.
Ottumwa: 100 Years. Scrapbook. Ottumwa Public Library.
Ottumwa History Including Diamond Jubilee Information.
        Scrapbook. Ottumwa Public Library.
Thrall, Seneca B., Civil War Letters, Sept. 1862 to May 5, 1864.
        Ottumwa Public Library.
Wapello County Scrapbook. Ottumwa Public Library.

maps and atlases

Illustrated Historical Atlas of the State of Iowa. Chicago:
        Andreas Atlas Co., 1875.
Map of Wisconsin Territory. Drawn in 1836 by Lt. Albert Lea,
        surveyor stationed with U.S. Dragoons.

periodicals

Mott, David C., "Abandoned Post Offices and Towns." *Annals
        of Iowa*, (Vol. XVII, 6, 7, 8 and Vol. XVIII, Nos. 1, 2, 3,
        1930-32): 132-134.
Wynes, Charles E., "Alexander the Great, Bridge Builder."
        Palimpest, Iowa's Popular History Magazine, (May/June
        1985): 78-86.

references

Baker, Chris D., compiler, *Wapello County History Index.*
        Ottumwa: Ottumwa Printing, 1991.

unpublished material

Doller, Eulalia, *Wapello County, Iowa, 1843 to 1877.*
        Manuscript, 1943.
Quinn, Tom, *Cigar Manufacturing in Ottumwa, Iowa: An 83-
        Year History.* Manuscript, 1989.

interviews

Mirgon, Ben, Ottumwa: March,1991.
Vivian, Carol, Ottumwa: January, 1992.
Robinson, Charles, Ottumwa: January, 1992.
Sharp, Mary and Allen, Ottumwa: August, 1991.
Stewart, Jo Moore, Atlanta: February, 1992.

index